AF133154

CENTREPIECE

CENTRE —PIECE

Bold, vibrant recipes to put vegetables in the spotlight

HELEN GRAHAM

hamlyn

Contents

Foreword by Jay Rayner — 6

Why Vegetables? — 8

How to Use this Book — 12

Pantry Items & Where to Find Them — 14

The Essentials — 18

The Meal Before the Meal
— 21

The Main Event
— 91

On the Side
— 147

Something Sweet
— 187

UK/US Terms — 218
Vegan Recipes — 218
Recipes that Can Be Made Vegan — 219

Index — 220
Thanks — 223
About the Author — 223

Foreword
by Jay Rayner

We don't talk enough about good taste when we talk about chefs. We often talk about technique and knife skills and precision. But none of those acquired talents are worth anything unless the person wielding them has good and unique taste. Helen Graham is blessed with exquisite taste. She approaches ingredients which, in lesser hands, could seem complicated and bullying, in a manner that makes them seem welcoming, even logical. She has a mellifluously named pantry of ingredients that operate together like a close family: of preserved lemons and sumac, of pomegranate molasses, tahini, agave syrup, Aleppo chilli flakes, amba and so much more. Of course, she follows in the footsteps of those who went before, most notably Yotam Ottolenghi, for whom she worked. But she takes it to new places. Helen Graham enables us to see ingredients in new ways.

Ah yes, ingredients. The headline on my 2019 review of Helen's cooking at the original Bubala in Spitalfields, where she first gave voice to her vibrant, hungry song, used the phrase 'exuberantly vegetarian'. That makes it sound like the plant-forward agenda was blatantly obvious from the moment I stepped through the door. It really wasn't. As Helen herself says, Bubala didn't present itself as a meat-free zone. Bubala is a Yiddish term of endearment, the word a grandmother might use for her grandchild. It speaks of the Ashkenazi Jewish background that both Helen and I share. But that menu read as if it pulled on another Jewish culinary tradition altogether, that of the Sephardim of the Mediterranean. Ashkenazi food is a redoubt against the bitter cold of Eastern European winters; Sephardi food is all sunlight and warmth, and that was what emanated from Helen's menu.

The fact that it was entirely vegetable-focused only became clear to me a few dishes in. Indeed, I recall asking for the menu back so I could check, running my finger down dish names, title by title. It struck me that night as a profound marker of just how far non-meat cookery has come in the UK and elsewhere. The fact is that, for too long, those of us who did not necessarily want to eat meat were very much treated as second-class citizens by a chef culture rigorously trained in a French culinary tradition that put a lump of animal protein in the middle of the plate and worked out from there. Too many vegetarians lived through the mushroom risotto years; for vegans, they were the stuffed pepper years. Both groups were at best an afterthought; at worst they were a downright annoyance.

But the world moves on. The rise of meat-free cookery has not just been a victory of politics or ethics but also of imagination. Surely beautiful aubergines, as heavy and purple as an opera house curtain, or butternut squash the orange of a dying sun, or the whole funky allium family could be promoted from side dish to main event? Could they not, as this book's title puts it, become the centrepiece? Yes, of course they could. But every brave new world needs its confident guide to lead the rest of us by the hand. Happily, we have the great Helen Graham.

Having moved on from Bubala, she now brings us this beautiful book. *Centrepiece* is not just a collection of terrific recipes, although it is very much that. Come for her way with hummus, and the fabulous Yemeni breads; stay for the Star Anise & Orange Braised Fennel, or the Pickled Aubergines & Tahini and so much else. It is, like all the best cookbooks, a new way of seeing the world, of understanding flavour, of engaging with that part of the pantry which, for too long, has been left behind. It is an expression of Helen Graham's exquisite taste. We're very lucky to have it.

Why Vegetables?

The aim of this book is to shift the role of the vegetables in your kitchen from supporting actor to star of the show by imbuing them with the main character energy they truly deserve.

This is an attitude I picked up from my time as executive chef of Bubala, a Middle Eastern-inspired vegetarian restaurant in London. When it first opened in 2019, the vegetarian food scene in London was pretty dismal: your options were either a bean burger or a wild mushroom risotto. Bubala actually didn't advertise itself as a vegetarian restaurant, so when the doors first opened, the general public seemed confused. Many walked out when they couldn't spot any meat on the menu; a few even emailed the restaurant to ask if we'd cook them a steak if they brought it in. But a bring-your-own-steak restaurant Bubala was not. We held fast, and sure enough, in came the next wave of customers, who didn't even fully register that it was a vegetarian restaurant at first, but were so bowled over by the bold, high-impact flavours they found, paired with the simple treatment of vegetables, that it seemed kind of irrelevant. For me, this is where the magic happened.

Let me be clear: I am not a vegetarian. I like to eat meat from time to time, mostly when I'm at a restaurant where I know how and from where the meat is sourced. When I'm eating at home, I'll spend my money on the best vegetables I can find and cook and present the produce in a way that champions it, just the way it is.

There's another reason why I came to cook with vegetables. Fourteen years ago, I was terrified of joining a professional kitchen. There were barely any female chef role models around, and I anticipated entering a very shouty and macho environment. Sadly, in my early experience, cooking with meat seemed to stoke that fire; there was so much bravado involved in searing the perfect steak or butchering whole beasts. As I moved through kitchens, I realized I wanted a softer, gentler environment, one in which I could filter out the kind of chefs who made me feel uncomfortable. A vegetarian kitchen attracts a disproportionate number of women. The environment is peaceful, light, fun and so creative; it is an entirely different energy, and a wholly different frame through which we can share and enjoy food. Working in a vegetable-focused kitchen brought me an incredible amount of joy.

Because of this ethos, I've been able to eschew some of the more bro-ish styles of cooking. There are no foams or gels or any ridiculous gadgets. I had a sous-vide machine very briefly, which I used as a (really expensive) timer. The recipes in this book are born out of this spirit of simplicity and require very little restaurant-level technique. They are simply direct expressions of very delicious vegetables.

You won't find any meat substitutes in this book. Sure, there's a time and a place for a veggie burger and fake meat, but that isn't here or now. I find those foods overly processed, though at the same time, cooking them feels oddly as though you're settling for second best. For too long, vegetarian food has been seen as a bit of an afterthought, and my aim in this book is to raise the stakes (pardon the pun) and show that, by cooking vegetables in the way you'll find here, you won't even think about meat. I'm also not out to tell you how to eat a balanced meal, get all your protein and fibre and so on. Anyone who knows me knows that a dietician I ain't. Truly, I am just here to tell you why vegetables are a really good time.

My cooking is playful and comes from a lifetime spent pinballing between the many facets of my Jewish identity. It comes from my Eastern European (Ashkenazi) heritage and stretches to the Sephardic lands of Iraq, Spain, North Africa and beyond, exploring food from the diaspora through friends, family and a whole load of travel.

Growing up, weekdays were spent eating my mum's delicious and comforting schnitzel and matzah ball soup at home. At the weekends, we were taken to the exotic land of Golders Green in North London, to all the kosher restaurants serving up Sephardic and Mizrahi cuisine, to enjoy hummus, shawarma, shakshuka and falafel. The contrast, to me, was striking, and I became really inspired by the juxtaposition. When I took my first chef job at The Palomar – a central London restaurant celebrating the food of the Middle East – back in 2014, I was blown away by the ingredients the chefs had at hand. There was fresh za'atar, amba (an Iraqi pickled mango sauce), various spice mixes and an abundance of herbs. This was so exciting to me, and was something I carried through to my vegetarian cooking when I joined Bubala. I wanted people to eat my food and feel that same sense of exhilaration and discovery.

However, all those spices, herbs and big flavours play supporting roles – though important ones – in the recipes that follow. Sadly, we don't usually see vegetables as having star quality, because we don't treat them in the same way as we do meat. They don't get the same level of care, the rich sauces or elaborate reductions. However, the second you do treat them in this way, you realize that, as with every cheesy romcom where the love interest takes off their glasses, the main character energy has been there all along.

Just like the vegetables in this book stepping into the spotlight, my own story begins when I stepped into the main character role of my life. From 2014 to 2018, I cooked at some of London's best Middle Eastern restaurants, as well as the Ottolenghi Test Kitchen, but eventually I burned out, as the restaurant industry leaves you with very little time for a social life. I then went on to spend five intense and exhilarating years as Executive Chef at Bubala, where the restaurant's success and growth from one location to two during my time there brought with it both immense pride and total exhaustion. Stepping away from it all felt terrifying but necessary.

When the opportunity to write this cookbook came along, it was accompanied by a quiet reawakening. As I tested each new recipe, I invited people over: friends, family, even strangers from Instagram. I wanted to see how the food worked in a real-life setting, how it brought people together. Watching that unfold sparked immeasurable joy and reminded me exactly why I cook.

Writing this book also made me ask a harder question: what makes a dish truly mine? Answering that meant drawing deeply from my personal history and the many cultural threads of my identity. In between recipes, I also finally had time to rediscover myself. I learned to swim, to surf, to forage; I made pottery and saw more live music. Who I really was at my core came more and more into focus and, as I was swimming one afternoon, I realized this book meant so much more to me than the reframing of how we serve and eat vegetables. It had led to me getting back to being the main character in my own life.

This book is an ode to that return – to family, to friends old and new, and to the magic of sharing food together. I hope that by cooking and enjoying these recipes you will discover in *Centrepiece* the same special moments I have enjoyed while writing it.

How to Use this Book

I feel a cookbook should be pretty self-explanatory, but here are a few notes to help guide you through.

—— Blending

The piece of kitchen equipment that works hardest for me is a high-powered bullet blender. I do pretty much everything in this: grinding all my spices (except saffron, which I do with a pestle and mortar), making hummus, pulsing nuts, smoothing sauces. In addition, because it is so powerful, it can generate the heat you need to make infused herb oils at a restaurant level, which is pretty cool, making it actually quite high-level kit, despite its size.

—— Veganizing dishes

More than half the recipes in this book are vegan. In another quarter of them, you can easily swap the ingredients listed to make them vegan. These recipes are marked, and there is also an index in the back of the book that shows which are vegan and which can be made vegan (see pages 218–19). I don't feel vegan yogurt offers the same sourness and mouthfeel as regular yogurt, which is why, for some yogurt recipes, I do not suggest a vegan option, as the balance in the overall dish would be off, but feel free to give it a go if you want. My favourite plant-based butter is Naturli: it contains all-natural, organic ingredients and behaves almost identically to dairy butter, with no synthetic aftertaste.

—— Presentation

Most of the recipes in this book are designed to be served on great big platters placed in the middle of the table, creating a really colourful and exciting spread. I love people to help themselves, and think it makes for a much more relaxing and congenial atmosphere as each person asks to be passed various bits and pieces. Guests can then eat as much or as little as they want without bothering the host, which means she or he can truly relax when they sit down. For this, I recommend investing in a few attractive platters. Most of the recipes contain instructions for which components can be made ahead, so much of the time it's simply a question of assembling dishes just before eating.

—— Live fire cooking

My preference is always to cook vegetables on live fire. However, this book is written knowing this is rarely possible. If you *do* have a barbecue on the go, dishes such as the Harissa Roast Carrots on page 122 would be even better for a lovely lick of smoke. If you are cooking any of the skewers (see pages 52, 61, 67, 74 and 88) over a live flame, the slower you can cook them, the better. Make sure that the flames have settled before you put the skewers on, and that you put them in a spot that's only mildly hot, turning regularly, so that the vegetables cook at the same pace as the marinades caramelize.

—— A note on desserts

Beyond vegetables, of course, there's room in this book for dessert. The running joke at Bubala was that there were only two desserts on the menu for the first three years, entirely owing to my total lack of patience with them. Understanding pastry is like being a scientist. You need a molecular comprehension of what makes things set too hard, too soft or not at all; you need to pay attention to temperature, and intuition gets you nowhere. Being a cook entirely guided by intuition, I was a bit of a disaster here. However, I've come up with a chapter of sweet recipes that are pretty robust, so if you are also someone who struggles with desserts, I got you.

Pantry Items
& Where to Find Them

Throughout the book, a few ingredients will pop up that you may not have in your kitchen. I want to tell you a little more about them, and why I think they should make it into your cupboard.

—— Agave syrup

A natural nectar derived from the agave plant that I use frequently in both sweet and savoury dishes. I prefer it to honey in savoury dishes, as it is both less overpowering and vegan-friendly. It's also far more affordable than maple syrup. You can, of course, opt for honey or maple syrup instead, though I'd use a little less than the recipe states and taste as you go. Agave syrup is available in most supermarkets.

—— Aleppo chilli flakes

Hailing from the region of Syria and Turkey, these chillies are often known as *pul biber*. The flakes have a slightly oily texture, which comes from being semi-dried and coarsely ground, so they are lovely to scatter over finished dishes. They don't bring the heat in the same way as regular chilli flakes; instead, what they offer is a deeper yet more subtle, fruity type of heat that is slightly more aromatic. You will find them in Middle Eastern grocers or online.

—— Amba

A pickled mango condiment from Iraq. Legend has it that the Jewish Sassoon family developed it after beginning to import India's beautiful mangos, which needed to be preserved in barrels of vinegar, hence amba's astringent and sour quality. Seasoned with turmeric and fenugreek, amba took on the flavours of Iraq but was soon adopted by neighbouring countries. In the Middle East, it's generally eaten on shawarma and falafel sandwiches, to add acidity against the rich tahini.

Being an absolute fiend for sour, tangy flavours, I have a slight obsession with amba. It's tricky to find, and the rare supermarket versions tend to be much too sweet, so I recommend you buy it online.

—— Ancho chilli flakes

Ancho chillies are dried poblano peppers from Mexico. These flakes have a deep, smoky, raisiny, chocolate-like flavour profile. Again, they are not that spicy, but they add a lot of smoky warmth to dishes. You can find them in some supermarkets. If not, you can use whole dried ancho chillies – just lightly toast them, remove the stalks and grind them into a coarse powder in a spice grinder or your most powerful blender – or just regular chilli flakes.

—— Black vinegar

This is from China, where you can find two types: one made with bran and the other from glutinous rice. I don't understand why this vinegar hasn't made it beyond the Chinese repertoire, as it is incredible: it has a deep, molasses flavour, with hints of liquorice and malt. It lacks the sharp acidity of other vinegars, instead offering a fuller sweet–sour experience, a bit like a deeply savoury pomegranate molasses. I love to pair it with bitter foods such as radicchio (see my Burnt Honey, Black Vinegar & Parmesan Radicchio on page 179), as it really makes them pop. You can find it at East Asian supermarkets or online. If you're based in the UK, you'll probably find Chinkiang vinegar, which is a personal favourite.

—— Curry leaves

Popular in South Asian and Sri Lankan cooking, these are not to be confused with curry powder (nor is curry powder an adequate substitute). Their flavour is citrussy, a bit like lemongrass, with notes of aniseed. I absolutely love them. They can be tricky to track down and are not generally available in most supermarkets, though I often find them in health food or organic shops. It is also possible to buy large bunches of the fresh leaves online. When I am lucky enough to come across them, I stock up and store them in my freezer, where they keep for a few months.

Date syrup

Ah, my true love, made simply by cooking down dates in water until they form a thick, molasses-like syrup. Date syrup is available in a few supermarkets and all good Middle Eastern stores. If you can find the Basra brand – which has Iraqi roots and comes in a jar – lucky you. This is probably the product I reach for most often in my kitchen. I pour it over most things, but especially yogurt, porridge and toast with tahini. It adds a deep treacle-like flavour to a lot of the savoury recipes in this book and I promise that, if you buy it, you will never choose to be without it again!

Dried limes

These sun-dried limes, otherwise known as black limes or *loomi*, originate from the Persian Gulf, Iraq and Iran. They add a floral, sour backnote to your cooking. Through the power of time and heat, the lime flavour is distilled into something like a natural citrus sherbet. I recommend investing in a bag; if you keep them in an airtight container, they will be good for a year or so. You can find them in your Middle Eastern store or online.

Fenugreek seeds

The dried seeds of the fenugreek plant are very bitter and nutty, but can be made slightly milder by gently toasting. Aside from their very distinctive flavour, fenugreek seeds have a thickening ability, as you'll discover if you make Lahoh (see page 44).

Harissa

A North African spice paste with amazing depth due to chillies and various spices, including caraway, coriander and cumin. The quality can vary massively and I'd avoid supermarket brands wherever possible and purchase something made in the Maghreb. My favourite of all time is a brand called Lamiri, produced in Tunisia using dried and smoked chillies. The flavour is unbelievable and having it in your arsenal is transformative, whether for the recipes in this book, just stirred into stews or marinades or even simply served with eggs.

Nigella seeds

It took me longer than I care to admit to realize that these do not have anything to do with Nigella Lawson (though if anyone deserves a spice dedicated to them, it's Nigella). This spice has different names depending on where you are in the world; you might know it as black cumin, onion seed or black caraway, which is weird, as it is none of these things. The seeds are a little bitter and because of this distinct flavour there's no need to grind them; they're just there in the background to add pops of treacly and deeply savoury contrast against sweet things such as my Leek, Miso & Mango Chutney Skewers (see page 67). These are available in most shops.

Orange blossom water

A byproduct of orange blossom distillation, this is a highly aromatic extract that is typically used to flavour sweets across the Middle East and East Africa, including baklava, semolina puddings and pastries, though Morocco uses it liberally in both sweet and savoury meals. I love the way it tempers sharper flavours, such as olives, tomatoes and feta in savoury dishes. It's in the pea salad on page 180, the sweet potatoes on page 144 and, more traditionally, the Zohar cake on page 196. You can generally find it in health food shops, as well as Middle Eastern grocers.

Pomegranate molasses

A syrup made by reducing pomegranate juice, this is a true staple of Middle Eastern food from Iran to Turkey via Lebanon and Syria. It is typically used in savoury dishes to add a sweet-and-sour flavour profile. You can find it in larger supermarkets, but also in any Middle Eastern grocery shop; just be sure to avoid any version with added sugar.

Saffron

There are a few recipes in this book that use saffron, which is, of course, the most expensive spice out there (oops, sorry). If you are going to invest in it, you'll want to extend the flavour of your saffron as much as possible. You can accomplish this by turning it into a fine powder with a pestle and mortar or spice grinder and then soaking it in hot water to create a very concentrated saffron liquid to add to a dish. You can also 'bloom' the whole saffron threads in hot water before using; you'll just end up with a less intense flavour. I've worked out how to circumnavigate this by making sauces a day in advance to give the saffron the chance to infuse as much flavour and colour as possible. When you stir my saffron custard (see page 212) or saffron tahini (see page 116) the next day, you'll see a deeper yellow colour ripple through the dish.

Sumac

The red, waxy ground berries of trees grown across the Levant and Turkey, sumac is zippy and sharp, adding a citrus freshness to dishes and lifting the flavour of anything it seasons. Wherever you would use a lemon – in salad dressings, seasonings for vegetables, finishing off a rich sauce – you can use sumac. Use it *in addition to* lemon and, wow, you've got something super-vibrant and fresh. Sumac is a *must must* must-have in your kitchen. Fortunately, it is stocked by several supermarkets. If you do ever get to browse the spice bazaars of the Middle East, you'll see many different grades; the more vividly coloured, fragrant and waxier, the better.

Tahini

A ground sesame paste available in most supermarkets. The quality varies tremendously, and investing in a high-quality tahini will have a huge impact on your dishes. Look out for a smooth, homogenous paste that's fairly pale in colour. Many cheaper brands will reveal themselves through split tahini paste in which the sesame oil and paste have separated because, when produced on a huge scale, the seeds are milled far too quickly. This often tastes bitter and is very difficult to mix back together, so cooking with it is pretty tricky. It's safer to avoid supermarket brands and buy tahini from a Middle Eastern store. Lebanese-made brands are great.

Vegan fish sauce

Actually a saline concentrate of soy and seaweed, this gives you a similar fishy hit to regular fish sauce. I find mine at organic health food shops, but you can use Maggi seasoning instead if it's too difficult to track down. If you're not vegetarian, just use regular fish sauce!

The Essentials

Ras el Hanout

This translates to 'head of the shop' or 'top shelf' from the Arabic, and if you walk into a spice shop in North Africa, it is a blend of their very best spices. The recipe therefore varies dramatically and each supermarket blend I've seen is different, so I wanted to provide a recipe for consistency. However, shop-bought blends are good too. Feel free to skip the dried rose petals if you are having trouble finding them, though they add a nice floral backnote to temper the paprika.

Makes about 6 tablespoons
—— Vegan

1½ tablespoons cumin seeds
1 tablespoon dried rose petals
1 tablespoon coriander seeds
½ tablespoon black peppercorns
2 tablespoons sweet paprika
½ tablespoon ground cinnamon

Using a spice grinder or high-powered bullet blender, blitz the cumin seeds, rose petals, coriander seeds and black peppercorns to a fine powder.

Tip into a small bowl and stir in the paprika and cinnamon.

Transfer to a clean jar and seal.

Preserved Lemons

Many recipes for preserved lemons call for them to be packed with salt alone. However, I like using oil *and* salt so that they lose their harsh astringency and become creamy with a punchy flavour. The oil also means they keep longer (for months in the fridge). You can use the whole lemon slices, skin, pith and all – hell, even the pips, which I never remove (life is too short).

Makes 1 large jar
—— Vegan

4 unwaxed lemons
1½ tablespoons sea salt flakes
200ml (7fl oz) neutral-flavoured oil, plus more if needed

First sterilize a 1-litre (1¾-pint) jar. Preheat the oven to 140°C fan (325°F), Gas Mark 3 and wash the jar thoroughly with hot, soapy water. Place it upright on a baking tray in the oven for 20 minutes, then turn off the oven, leaving the jar in there until you're ready to use it.

Slice the lemons as finely as possible, discarding the ends. Layer them into the jar, sprinkling each layer with a little salt. The lemons can overlap slightly, but you're aiming to expose as much flesh as possible to the salt.

Pour over the oil, ensuring all the lemons are submerged.

Tear a piece of nonstick baking paper the same size as the top of the jar and press it over the lemons, seal with the lid and transfer to the fridge. After 4 days, the lemons will be ready to use.

Hawaij

Throughout this book you will hear of my love for Yemeni food, which was introduced to me via Jews hailing from Yemen, and hawaij is one of its bedrocks: an earthy spice mix traditionally used in soups and stews. Make it. Keep it in your cupboard. Use it for my recipes. But also toss veg in it before roasting, or stir it through yogurt to serve on the side too. It is one of the most enlivening spice mixes I know. It isn't something you can easily buy, so I recommend making it yourself.

Makes about 6 tablespoons
— *Vegan*

2 tablespoons black peppercorns
2 tablespoons cumin seeds
10 cloves
1 tablespoon coriander seeds
1 tablespoon ground turmeric
¼ teaspoon ground cardamom

Using a spice grinder or high-powered bullet blender, blitz the black peppercorns, cumin seeds, cloves and coriander seeds to a fine powder.

Tip out into a small bowl and stir in the turmeric and cardamom.

Transfer to a clean jar and seal.

Baharat

This is a really warming, wintry spice mix that I employ generally to accompany earthy flavours; it's great on root vegetables, providing smoky complexity. The word *baharat* simply means 'spices' in Arabic, but that translation does this mix a huge injustice, as its ability to add both subtle smoky spice and sweetness means it can do some serious heavy lifting in a dish that's otherwise quite simple. I especially love it in the Butternut Squash, Baharat Candied Chestnuts & Whipped Feta (see page 119).

Makes about 5 tablespoons
— *Vegan*

1 tablespoon cumin seeds
1 teaspoon black peppercorns
6 cloves
½ teaspoon caraway seeds
¼ teaspoon cardamom seeds (not the pods)
2 tablespoons sweet smoked paprika
1 tablespoon ground cinnamon
½ teaspoon ground nutmeg

Using a spice grinder or high-powered bullet blender, blitz the cumin seeds, black peppercorns, cloves and caraway and cardamom seeds to a fine powder.

Tip into a small bowl and stir in the paprika, cinnamon and nutmeg. Transfer to a clean jar and seal.

The Meal Before the Meal

Caramelized Courgette Dip
with Dates & Fenugreek

When you cook courgettes low and slow in plenty of olive oil, they begin to disintegrate, caramelize and become very sweet. This recipe takes a lot of oil, but the courgettes absorb much of it and you won't get that deep flavour without it. You can't really taste the coconut here; it just binds the courgette to create something creamy but surprisingly light.

Serves 4
—— *Vegan*

135ml (4¾fl oz) olive oil, plus 2 tablespoons to serve
1kg (2lb 4oz) courgettes, sliced into 3mm (⅛-inch) rounds (a mandoline is best for this)
1½ teaspoons fine sea salt
1 teaspoon ground fenugreek seeds
100g (3½oz) pitted medjool dates, finely chopped
5 garlic cloves, finely grated
1 teaspoon Aleppo chilli flakes, plus a pinch to serve
250ml (9fl oz) coconut cream
2 tablespoons lemon juice

For the garnish
1 tablespoon pine nuts, toasted
handful of mint leaves

Put the oil in a large frying pan set over a medium heat. Add your sliced courgettes, salt and fenugreek and gently sauté for about 1½ hours, stirring regularly, until the courgettes disintegrate and form a darkly coloured mass.

Meanwhile, soak the dates in a small bowl of hot water for 10 minutes, then drain and set aside.

Stir the dates, garlic and Aleppo chilli into the courgette pan and sauté for a further 2 minutes until the garlic is fragrant. Pour in the coconut cream, stir, then allow to simmer for 5 minutes, stirring every so often, until most of the coconut has evaporated and its aroma has cooked off. You'll be left with a very creamy, thick courgette paste. Turn off the heat and stir in the lemon juice. Transfer to a bowl and allow to cool completely.

Spread the dip on to a serving plate, drizzle with the olive oil and sprinkle with the extra Aleppo chilli, the pine nuts and mint.

—— **How to serve**

I especially like this scooped up with something contrastingly crispy, such as pitta chips.

Labneh

A strained yogurt eaten across the Middle East, this is sour and tangy and belongs in any mezze spread, either as is, perhaps sprinkled with olive oil and za'atar or with one of the toppings on pages 26-7 if you're feeling adventurous. I go for the Fage brand 5% fat yogurt here, as it's already very thick and sour and ensures a luxurious-feeling labneh. It also loses less whey than other brands, so you get a better yield.

Makes 600g (1lb 5oz) / Serves 6

950g (2lb 2oz) 5% fat Greek yogurt (see recipe introduction)
1 teaspoon fine sea salt

The night before you want the labneh, whisk the yogurt and salt together in a bowl until fully combined.

Place a colander over a separate bowl and line it with a clean tea towel. Tip the yogurt into this, then fold over the tea towel to fully cover the contents. Place a heavy bowl directly on the cloth-wrapped yogurt, then transfer to the fridge overnight.

Decant your labneh into a container the following day and it's ready to use.

Things to Have with Labneh

Confit Tomatoes, Hawaij & Crispy Basil

The combination of tomatoes and labneh is just the best. Sweet and sour, they complement each other so well, while hawaij elevates this topping to something special. Crispy basil makes this look beautiful, but you can scatter over fresh basil leaves and skip the frying part, if you prefer.

Serves 4 as a topping for labneh
—— **Vegan**

70ml (2$\frac{1}{3}$fl oz) olive oil
leaves from 30g (1oz) basil
1 teaspoon fine sea salt, plus more for the fried basil
4 garlic cloves, finely sliced
500g (1lb 2oz) cherry tomatoes
1 tablespoon hawaij (for homemade, see page 19)
½ tablespoon nigella seeds

Heat the olive oil in a small saucepan. Line a plate with kitchen paper and grab a slotted spoon. Once the oil is hot, drop in half the basil leaves and stir and fry until they turn translucent; this will only take 20-30 seconds, so be ready with that spoon. Once it is ready, scoop the basil out on to the prepared plate and sprinkle with a little salt. Repeat with the second batch of basil leaves, then set aside.

Turn the heat to medium-low, add the garlic and fry for 2 minutes until fragrant, then add the tomatoes, hawaij and the 1 teaspoon of salt. Stir and gently simmer for 15-20 minutes or until the tomatoes have softened and their skins have split. Turn off the heat and allow to cool.

Smooth your labneh on to a serving dish and spoon over the tomatoes and some of that lovely flavoured oil. Sprinkle over the nigella seeds and crispy basil and serve.

Peach, Curry Leaf & Coconut

This is inspired by a holiday to Sri Lanka. After a few weeks surfing with friends, I travelled the southern coast until I settled in Hiriketiya, the most beautiful little bay. Somehow over dinner on my first night I was talked into doing a pop-up at that restaurant on the next! I drunkenly crafted a menu and the chef promised to head off on his motorbike to forage for fresh rambutans, curry leaves, pandan, local *kithul* treacle and curd, a very tangy set buffalo milk sold in beautiful clay pots, which reminded me of labneh. Cooking with these new ingredients was a revelation and this salsa, served on labneh, is so evocative of the meal I cooked that night.

Serves 4 as a topping for labneh
—— *Vegan*

4 tablespoons olive oil
2 garlic cloves, finely sliced
2 tablespoons desiccated coconut
1 teaspoon black mustard seeds
30 fresh curry leaves
2 tablespoons lime juice
1 teaspoon chilli powder
1½ tablespoons agave syrup, or maple syrup
½ teaspoon fine sea salt
3 ripe peaches, stoned, each cut into 16 slices

—— **How to serve**

Eat this with a pile of hot flatbreads, alongside Hummus and Moutabal (see pages 36–7 and 33) for a lovely spread.

Place the oil in a saucepan over a low heat. This cooks very *very* quickly, so keep a bowl next to the hob ready to decant the cooked mix into, as it continues to cook off the heat. Add the sliced garlic to the oil and fry for 1–2 minutes until it is beginning to colour on the very edges. Add the coconut, mustard seeds and curry leaves and fry for a further minute or so until the curry leaves have crisped and the mustard seeds have taken on a slightly deeper colour. Decant straight away into the bowl and immediately stir in the lime juice, chilli powder, agave syrup and salt.

Add the peaches to this marinade and toss to coat. Leave them to macerate for at least 30 minutes before smoothing your labneh on to a serving dish and topping with the peaches and their dressing.

The Meal Before the Meal

Garlic Butter Malawach

Yemeni breads are exceptional and these layered breads are a staple. I've added plenty of garlic butter for an even more indulgent flaky, crispy experience. You can make these ahead of time and freeze them before cooking, separating them with sheets of nonstick baking paper. Fry them directly from frozen, to make for the crispiest malawach. These are also great with Basil Zhoug (see page 47) along with the Grated Tomatoes.

Makes 8
—— *Can be made vegan*

400g (14oz) plain flour, plus more to dust
270ml (9½fl oz) boiling water
1½ teaspoons fine sea salt
1½ teaspoons caster sugar
1½ teaspoons baking powder
vegetable oil, to oil and fry
Grated Tomatoes (see page 47), to serve

For the garlic butter
150g (5½oz) unsalted butter, or vegan butter
2 garlic cloves, finely chopped
¼ teaspoon fine sea salt
bunch of spring onions, trimmed and finely sliced
1 tablespoon toasted sesame seeds
1 tablespoon nigella seeds

Add the flour into a large mixing bowl. Put the measured boiling water, salt, sugar and baking powder in a jug, give a little whisk to combine, then add to the flour, using a wooden spoon to stir the dough until it feels cool enough to handle. It should be not too wet and quite rollable. Lightly flour a work surface and knead the dough for 10 minutes until it forms a smooth and pliable ball. Cover with a damp cloth and leave for 30 minutes.

Knead again for a further 5 minutes, then allow to rest for another 30 minutes, covered, in a lightly oiled bowl.

Once your dough has rested, divide it into 8 × 80g (2¾oz) pieces, rolling each into a round ball. Allow to rest on an oiled tray, again covered by a damp cloth.

For the garlic butter, put the butter, garlic and salt in a saucepan, set over a medium heat and stir until just melted, then set aside.

Lightly flour a work surface, pick up a dough ball (leave the others under the cloth) and roll it out as thinly as possible to roughly 15cm (6 inches) in diameter. Lightly brush this with the garlic butter, then roll it up from bottom to top into a tight sausage. Form this into a coil, tucking the end underneath. Roll out again into a 15cm (6-inch) circle and repeat the process twice more so that there are 3 layers of garlic butter. Repeat with the remaining dough balls.

Once each malawach is complete, put it on a plate, separating each with a sheet of nonstick baking paper.

Set the remaining garlic butter over a medium heat and add the spring onions, sesame seeds and nigella seeds. Stir and heat gently until the spring onions have softened; 3-4 minutes. Turn off the heat and leave somewhere warm until you're ready to serve.

Put 2 tablespoons of oil into a frying pan set over a medium heat, add a bread and fry until golden and crisp; about 2 minutes on each side. If it darkens too quickly, reduce the heat. Continue until all the breads are cooked, adding about 2 tablespoons of oil each time. This may seem a lot, but the breads need it to puff up.

Transfer the breads to a large serving dish and serve with the warm garlic butter and grated tomatoes in dishes alongside.

—— *How to serve*

I like this as a breakfast spread, to which you can add Tahini Sauce (see page 46) and boiled eggs to make it more substantial.

Moutabal & Lime Leaf Dressing

Cooking aubergines *properly* makes the difference between silky, smoky deliciousness and something bitter and rubbery, so err on the side of caution and cook them more than you think. An aubergine is grilled enough when it's a slippery slop that's unable to hold its own shape, aka burned to absolute and complete submission. Lime leaf lifts this and makes it a little more unexpected, but curry leaves also work nicely in their place.

Serves 4 as a starter
—— *Vegan*

4 aubergines
90g (3¼oz) coconut yogurt, or regular Greek yogurt
100g (3½oz) tahini
2 garlic cloves, finely grated
1 teaspoon ground cumin
50ml (2fl oz) lemon juice
1 teaspoon fine sea salt
4 tablespoons water
5g (⅛oz) mint leaves, to garnish (optional)

For the lime leaf dressing
5 lime leaves
50ml (2fl oz) olive oil
1 tablespoon lime juice
10g (¼oz) toasted coconut flakes
40g (1½oz) cashew nuts, toasted and roughly chopped
½ teaspoon Aleppo chilli flakes, or regular chilli flakes
½ tablespoon pomegranate molasses
½ teaspoon agave syrup
¼ teaspoon fine sea salt

Begin by grilling the aubergines. If you have a gas hob, set 2 rings on high and use a fork to pierce each aubergine 2–3 times so that the steam can escape. Place directly on to the flames and use tongs to rotate them every 5 minutes until they are completely soft and collapsed. To achieve this, you really need to take it there. Be brave, be fearless and don't remove the aubergines until they can barely hold their own form; the skins should be white when you remove them from the heat. If you don't have a gas hob, preheat the oven to 200°C fan (425°F), Gas Mark 7. Roast the aubergines on a rack in the upper one-third of the oven for 50–60 minutes until soft and squishy.

Once the aubergines are cooked, transfer to a colander set over a bowl to drain. Once cool, peel and discard the skins. Return the aubergines to the colander and press down with a ladle to extract as much moisture as possible, then roughly chop.

Put the yogurt in a large bowl with the tahini, garlic, cumin, lemon juice, salt and measured water and whisk to combine. Add the drained aubergine and stir thoroughly.

To make the dressing, if you have a high-powered bullet blender, use it to blend the lime leaves and oil together until it feels hot to the touch and the oil is a vivid green; this will take about 3 minutes. You can also do this in the small bowl of a regular blender: just blitz until the lime leaf is finely chopped and the colour of the oil has darkened a little to pale green. Strain into a bowl, discard the solids and allow to cool for 10 minutes, then stir in the remaining ingredients.

To serve, smooth the moutabal on to a serving dish and spoon over the dressing, scattering with mint leaves to garnish, if you like.

The Meal Before the Meal

Hummus
is a feeling

I'd love to know how much hummus I've made throughout my career; it could probably be measured by the metric tonne. Sometimes I think I *am* hummus. The most important thing I have learned is that your chickpeas must be as soft as possible, which means pre-soaking the pulses is vital, as is the addition of bicarbonate of soda, which helps break them down.

My first sous chef at Bubala, Jake Norman, always urged our chefs to go with their instincts when making hummus. After observing them work, I saw Jake was correct: things tended to go south when the chefs adhered to a recipe and ignored their intuition. The truth – discovered after years of cooking vast cauldrons of chickpeas – is that no batch is ever really the same. In the summer, soaked chickpeas are much more plump and almost dissolve into their cooking water after only 40 minutes or so, whereas chickpeas soaked during the winter months would still be hard, taking up to four hours to cook. Sometimes, in a fit of frustration that the chickpeas were not behaving as the recipe had told them, the chefs would pull the chickpeas off the heat while half-cooked, producing a grainy, sandy hummus that no amount of reblending could fix.

Sick of this, Jake rewrote the recipe, turning it into one of those cryptic codes they use as a Technical Challenge on *The Great British Bake Off*. 'Hummus is a feeling,' Jake proclaimed. Chefs were told to cook the chickpeas until they were done, and 'Blitz into a pillowy cloud of peng' was the new method. It's quite amazing how much people's cooking improves when you say: 'I trust you, you've got this. You don't need me or a recipe to tell you when they're cooked. You'll know. You know so much more than you think.'

Chefs moved through the kitchen with a new air of confidence, conferring with each other about the state of their chickpeas, but also trusting themselves so much more, taking ownership of their food and sharing their intuition with the rest of the team. It was one of the best things we did and, in turn, it shifted the whole culture of the kitchen.

Hummus

This is not a recipe but a guide. Recipes can be scary. They can be limiting. Cookbooks were not always as precise as they are now; precision is a new thing. I am sure there is a direct correlation between people saying they don't know how to cook and recipes becoming more exacting. So, here I present just a rough blueprint for making hummus.

Makes 800g (1lb 12oz) / Serves 6–8
—— **Vegan**

150g (5½oz) dried chickpeas
½ teaspoon bicarbonate of soda
2 garlic cloves, roughly chopped
1½ teaspoons ground cumin
2 teaspoons fine sea salt
70ml (2⅓fl oz) lemon juice
160g (5¾oz) tahini, plus more if needed

The night before you want to make your hummus, put the chickpeas in a large container or bowl and cover liberally with cold water. There should be a lot of water, and there should also be a lot of room for the chickpeas to double or triple in size. Soak for at least 8 hours. Don't skip this. Yes, they will cook if you boil them from unsoaked, but they will never be soft in the same way as pre-soaked chickpeas are.

Drain the chickpeas, transfer to a large saucepan and cover with at least 5cm (2 inches) of fresh cold water, plus the bicarbonate of soda. Set the saucepan over a medium-high heat. You can salt the water here if you like. It doesn't affect the chickpeas' softness, but it does inhibit your control over how salty the hummus will be, so I salt only when blending at the end. Stir and bring to the boil, then reduce the heat to a gentle simmer.

While the chickpeas are boiling, a scum will form on the surface of the water, which is all their impurities. Skim this off with a ladle or a slotted spoon and cook for 45 minutes or so before checking to see how soft the chickpeas are by running a few under cold water, then seeing if you can squish them between your fingers. If they squish easily and with little resistance, they're done, but you do need to keep cooking them until they're this soft. The time is just a guide here, as it's taken me anything from 45 minutes to 3 hours in the past (though they're generally cooked after 1½ hours).

As you are cooking the chickpeas, from maybe the 40-minute mark, you can go into the saucepan with a slotted spoon, disrupt the chickpeas and pull out any floating skins. The more skins you collect, the smoother the hummus will be, and it's definitely easier to do this once they have cooked for some time. Once they are fully cooked, before draining, you can turn off the heat and continue pulling out skins until you've got as many as you can get, or can be bothered to. (If you have a very powerful blender, this process won't matter so much, but if not, it's definitely a good idea.)

Place a colander over a bowl and drain your chickpeas, reserving their stock and then allowing both stock and chickpeas to cool separately; I'd leave them for at least 30 minutes. The reason I like to cool the chickpeas before making hummus is that, when they're hot, they absorb much more liquid, meaning you end up with a much stiffer hummus than you'd want. How the texture is when you make it from cooled chickpeas is how the texture will stay.

To blend the hummus, you want the most powerful blender you have. My blender of choice is a high-powered bullet blender, but in lieu of that, you want the type you'd use to make a smoothie. Put the chickpeas into that blender with 300ml (½ pint) of the cooking liquid, the garlic, cumin and salt. The cooking liquid will be a dark brown and a little viscous, but still pourable. If there was too little water in the pot when the chickpeas were cooking, it will have a viscous jelly-like texture, so if this is the case, just whisk in a little cold water to loosen it. Blend until the mix resembles a really thick but completely smooth smoothie. To achieve this, you may have to blend it for a good few minutes. If it's feeling a little stiff, add some more cooking stock.

Decant into a bowl and whisk in the lemon juice and tahini. If you want it thicker, add more tahini, and if you want it looser, add more stock.

How to serve

Hummus is pretty perfect just the way it is and you can serve it with plenty of good olive oil (mandatory), za'atar or hot paprika, or even sumac. On pages 40–1, you will find three flavoured oils that I like to pour over my hummus when I am serving it for a group and want to make it extra-special.

Things to Have with Hummus

Má là Oil

This comes from a friend, chef Gal Ben Moshe, who used it in a dish at his central London residency. I was hooked, and it is incredible on hummus. *Má là* means numbing and spicy, and is a flavour profile prevalent in Sichuanese food. I love how this recipe uses Mexican chillies for a layer of smoky complexity against the numbing heat of the Sichuan peppercorns. They may be tough to track down, but this recipe will last you through at least two batches of hummus, which makes the search a little more worthwhile.

Makes about 200ml (7fl oz)
—— *Vegan*

30g (1oz) dried mulato chillies, or guajillo chillies
1 teaspoon cumin seeds
1 teaspoon fennel seeds
1 teaspoon Sichuan peppercorns
2 garlic cloves, finely chopped
1 tablespoon finely chopped fresh root ginger
2 star anise
½ tablespoon caster sugar
1 tablespoon toasted sesame seeds
½ teaspoon fine sea salt
200ml (7fl oz) neutral-flavoured oil

Set a frying pan over a medium heat and add the dried chillies, lightly toasting for a minute or 2 on each side until fragrant. Set aside to cool before removing and discarding the stalks and seeds. Tear the chillies roughly and add to a spice grinder or bullet blender with the cumin and fennel seeds and Sichuan peppercorns. Blitz to a fine powder, then tip into a heatproof bowl with the garlic, ginger, star anise, sugar, sesame seeds and salt. Stir to combine.

Pour the oil into a saucepan and set over a high heat until it reaches or 180°C (356°F). If you don't have a temperature gun or probe thermometer, heat until smoking then turn off and leave to cool for 5 minutes. Pour the oil over the spice blend, stir thoroughly and allow to cool. Transfer to a sterilized jar (see page 18), seal and keep in the fridge.

—— **How to serve**

As well as on hummus, I love this on noodles, smashed cucumbers or stir-fried greens, drizzled over soups, Labneh (see page 24) or you could even try it over vanilla ice cream if you were feeling a little freaky…

Simple Sesame Oil

This takes minutes to pull together with just a few store-cupboard ingredients.

Makes about 100ml (3½fl oz), enough for 1 batch of Hummus
—— Vegan

1 tablespoon Aleppo chilli flakes, or regular chilli flakes
1 tablespoon black sesame seeds, toasted
1 tablespoon white sesame seeds, toasted
1 teaspoon sweet smoked paprika
1 teaspoon soy sauce
1 teaspoon maple syrup
2 garlic cloves, finely chopped
¼ teaspoon fine sea salt
100ml (3½fl oz) neutral-flavoured oil
2 star anise
1 cinnamon stick

Put the chilli flakes, sesame seeds, paprika, soy sauce, maple syrup, garlic and salt in a small heatproof bowl. Put the oil, star anise and cinnamon stick in a saucepan set over a low heat. Allow the spices to infuse gently for 8–10 minutes, swirling occasionally, until the oil is aromatic. Remove from the heat and strain over the sesame mixture. Stir well and let cool before use.

—— **How to serve**
When I'm not pouring this over my hummus, it's lovely in bowls of stir-fried greens, or over fried eggs.

Rosemary, Caraway & Ancho

This is such a nice combination and very little fuss to prepare.

Makes about 100ml (3½fl oz), enough for 1 batch of Hummus
—— Vegan

100ml (3½fl oz) neutral-flavoured oil
½ red onion, sliced into thin crescents
leaves from 3 rosemary sprigs
½ teaspoon caraway seeds
1 tablespoon ancho chilli flakes
¼ teaspoon hot smoked paprika
¼ teaspoon fine sea salt

Put the oil, red onion, rosemary, caraway seeds and chilli flakes in a small saucepan. Simmer over a medium heat for about 10 minutes until the onion is soft and beginning to brown. Turn off the heat, pour the oil into a heatproof bowl and stir in the paprika and salt. Allow to cool before use.

—— **How to serve**
As well as over hummus, this is great drizzled on top of roasted carrots and pumpkin.

Matbucha
with Jalapeño & Coriander

A North African tomato and red pepper dip in which peppers are slowly cooked to sweet, jammy total submission (the only way to eat red peppers, except if you're suffering from a desperate nutrient deficiency and need to wolf one down raw). At home, we would enjoy a Sunday morning spread of bagels and smoked salmon alongside matbucha, hummus and pickled herring.

Serves 4-6
—— **Vegan**

100ml (3½fl oz) olive oil
4 red peppers, cored, deseeded and cut into in 3cm (1¼-inch) pieces
1 teaspoon fine sea salt, plus more if needed
4 garlic cloves, finely sliced
1 jalapeño chilli, halved lengthways and finely sliced
1 teaspoon ground cumin
1 teaspoon sweet smoked paprika
¼ teaspoon cayenne pepper
400g (14oz) can of chopped tomatoes
2 teaspoons caster sugar
flatbreads, to serve

For the jalapeño & coriander salsa
2 jalapeño chillies, halved lengthways, deseeded and finely chopped
30g (1oz) coriander, chopped
4 tablespoons olive oil
2 tablespoons lemon juice
½ teaspoon fine sea salt

Put the oil in a nonstick saucepan and set it over a medium-low heat. Add the peppers and salt and gently sauté for 45 minutes, stirring regularly, until they have collapsed and become squishy and their skins begin to peel away.

Stir in the garlic, jalapeño, cumin, paprika and cayenne and sauté for a further 10 minutes until the garlic becomes translucent.

Add the canned tomatoes and cook gently for another 25-30 minutes, stirring regularly, until almost all the moisture has evaporated. Turn off the heat, stir in the sugar and check for salt, then set aside to cool.

Meanwhile, mix together all the ingredients for the salsa in a small bowl.

Transfer the cooled matbucha to a serving plate and serve topped with the salsa, along with flatbreads.

—— **How to serve**

Matbucha is lovely as a cold dip, but can also be turned into a shakshuka sauce by letting it down with a little water. Once you've cooked your shakshuka, the jalapeño and coriander salsa is delicious spooned on top of the eggs too.

Lahoh

Spongy pancake-like breads eaten across Yemen and East Africa, these have been adopted by Yemenite Jews across the diaspora, which is how I discovered them. If you've had *injera*, these are similar, with fenugreek giving sourness to the fermented batter. They're honestly great whenever you want bread for dipping or mopping-up sauces, as their texture allows them to absorb all the flavours.

Makes 10
—— **Vegan**

380g (13oz) plain flour
2 teaspoons fine sea salt
7g (¼oz) sachet of fast-action dried yeast
1 teaspoon ground fenugreek seeds
760ml (1¼ pints) lukewarm water

Put all the ingredients in a bowl and whisk thoroughly to combine, ensuring there are absolutely no lumps. It should be the consistency of regular pancake batter.

Cover and leave in a warm place to rise. This will take around 2 hours, depending on how warm the room is; you want the batter to be doubled in size, bubbly, poofy and a little gloopy from the fenugreek.

Once the batter is ready, set a 28cm (11-inch) nonstick frying pan over a medium-high heat. Whisk your batter to deflate the bubbles. Once the pan is hot, add a ladle of the batter (about 110ml/3¾fl oz), tilting the pan so that it spreads evenly to the edges. Bubbles will start to form on top, a bit like a crumpet. Fry for 1–2 minutes until the top is completely dry and matt. The bottom should not colour too much, so reduce the heat if it is looking a little dark. These only cook on one side, so it's important to make sure they're completely dry on top before removing from the pan.

Once the lahoh are cooked, use a fish slice to transfer them to a plate, stacking them on top of each other as you go. You can serve them straight away.

—— **How to serve**

These are lovely with Tahini Sauce, Basil Zhoug and Grated Tomatoes (see pages 46 and 47), but wonderful served sweet too, with jam and butter for breakfast, or warmed through with maple syrup.

Essential sauces

Tahini Sauce

Just as with hummus, making good tahini sauce is a feeling. Essentially, this recipe is a guide, here for emotional support, as making this can be a little fraught. Tahini paste plays tricks on you: it likes to split when liquid is introduced. Early in my career I'd freak out when this happened, possibly even chuck it away, but it's absolutely normal. Have a little faith. Tahini paste is high in fat, so any liquid needs to be introduced very slowly, whisking continuously. If it does seize, just continue to add liquid… it will sort itself out eventually. Each jar of tahini paste is different, so add more water or more tahini to get the right consistency, which should be like a thick pancake batter.

Serves 4
—— Vegan

220g (7¾oz) tahini
160ml (5¾fl oz) cold water
2 tablespoons lemon juice
½ tablespoon fine sea salt

Put the tahini in a mixing bowl and slowly whisk in enough of the measured water to reach the consistency of thick pancake batter. Whisk in the lemon juice and salt.

This can be stored for 3 days in the fridge.

Basil Zhoug

Zhoug is a Yemeni coriander sauce containing hawaij spice mix. Don't skip the hawaij here; it's absolutely non-negotiable for zhoug. You can find a recipe for the spice mix on page 19.

Serves 4 with breads for dipping
—— *Vegan*

2 garlic cloves, roughly chopped
1 green chilli, roughly chopped
30g (1oz) basil, roughly chopped
30g (1oz) coriander, roughly chopped
100ml (3½fl oz) olive oil
2 tablespoons lemon juice
1 teaspoon hawaij (for homemade, see page 19)
½ teaspoon fine sea salt

Put the garlic and chilli in a blender and roughly chop.

Add the remaining ingredients and blend until smooth and emulsified but retaining some texture; you still want to see some flecks of herbs.

—— *How to serve*

If you want something bright and vibrant to go on your hummus, this is your ticket. But zhoug is far more than just 'something for hummus' and it deserves a spot at your table alongside Malawach or Lahoh with Hummus, Tahini Sauce and so on (see pages 28, 44, 36-7 and opposite). Basil Zhoug makes everything better, and it also features in my potato salad (see page 154).

Grated Tomatoes

This is barely a recipe but is something that absolutely had to be included in this book. It is the ying to tahini's yang – the acidic contrast to tahini's richness – and I always serve the two alongside each other with fresh bread. Being so simple, this relies heavily on the quality of the tomatoes, so try to pick ones that are really ripe and juicy.

Serves 8
—— *Vegan*

500g (1lb 2oz) vine tomatoes
1 tablespoon olive oil
1 tablespoon lemon juice
½ teaspoon fine sea salt

Cut the tomatoes in half horizontally, then grate the exposed flesh on the coarse side of a cheese grater into a large bowl. Discard the skins and gently tip away any excess liquid from the tomatoes.

Stir in the olive oil, lemon juice and salt.

The Meal Before the Meal

Cumin Aubergine & Coriander Chutney
with Star Anise Caramel

Both the coriander chutney and the caramel here can be made ahead. However, make sure you cook the aubergines fresh because their crisp, slightly chewy texture against these sauces is so, so good. Undercooked aubergine can wreck a dish. Make sure you cook them to the point of collapse when given a little prod, resulting in a soufflé-like texture within.

Serves 4 as a small plate
—— **Vegan**

2 aubergines
4 tablespoons olive oil
1 teaspoon fine sea salt
½ tablespoon ground cumin

For the star anise caramel
75ml (2½fl oz) light soy sauce
75g (2¾oz) caster sugar
3 star anise

For the coriander chutney
100g (3½oz) coriander, roughly chopped
3 garlic cloves, roughly chopped
70ml (2⅓fl oz) olive oil
1 green chilli, roughly chopped
1 tablespoon vegan fish sauce
25ml (1fl oz) rice vinegar
1 teaspoon agave syrup
2 teaspoons lime juice
½ teaspoon fine sea salt
½ teaspoon Aleppo chilli flakes

Preheat the oven to 200°C fan (425°F), Gas Mark 7. Line a baking tray with nonstick baking paper.

To prepare the aubergines, remove the stalk ends, then cut the aubergines in half horizontally, then again vertically. Cut each quarter into 3 wedges. Place these in a large mixing bowl, add the oil, salt and cumin and toss thoroughly with your hands so that the seasoning is evenly distributed. Transfer to the lined tray and bake for 35 minutes, turning once halfway through, until totally cooked through and golden.

For the caramel, put all the ingredients in a small saucepan and bring to a simmer. Let it gently bubble away for about 3 minutes until a little reduced and syrupy. To test the consistency, dip a spoon into the caramel and let it cool for a few seconds. It should coat the back of the spoon and slowly drip off, rather than running off quickly. Transfer to a small heatproof bowl and set aside. If you suspect you've gone too far and it is a little over-reduced, you can take it off the heat and whisk in a little water until you get a looser consistency.

Put all the ingredients for the coriander chutney in a blender and blitz until fully combined and emulsified, but be careful not to over-blend, as you still want to see flecks of coriander.

Smooth the coriander chutney onto serving dishes. Spoon the aubergine on top – I sometimes stack it in a single line down the centre – then pour the caramel over the aubergine before serving.

Curry Leaf & Sumac Ezme

Ezme is a non-negotiable order at a Turkish restaurant and is perfect mopped up with flatbreads toasted on the grill. Mine is by no means a traditional version (like almost everything in this book), but it offers the classic *ezme* tang and spice with chilli and pomegranate molasses. The addition of curry leaves, allspice and lime juice gives it something playful and unexpected, especially as this dish looks rather inconspicuous.

Serves 4
—— **Vegan**

For the curry leaf & sumac dressing
75ml (2½fl oz) olive oil
40 fresh curry leaves
3 tablespoons pomegranate molasses
1½ teaspoons fine sea salt
2 teaspoons sumac
1 teaspoon ground allspice
1 tablespoon agave syrup
1 tablespoon lime juice
1 garlic clove, finely chopped

For the ezme salad
300g (10½oz) Turkish peppers (*sivri*), cored, deseeded and finely chopped (regular green peppers are also fine)
1 red onion, finely chopped
500g (1lb 2oz) vine tomatoes, deseeded and finely chopped
30g (1oz) parsley, finely chopped, plus 1 tablespoon to garnish
finely grated zest and juice of 1 unwaxed lime
1 red chilli, halved lengthways, deseeded and finely chopped

To make the dressing, if you have a high-powered bullet blender, use it to blend the oil and curry leaves until it feels hot to the touch and the oil is a vivid green; this will take about 3 minutes. You can also do this in the small bowl of a regular blender: just blitz until the curry leaves are finely chopped and the colour of the oil has darkened a little to pale green.

Strain the oil into a bowl, discarding the sediment. Whisk in the remaining dressing ingredients until thoroughly incorporated and emulsified.

Mix all the ingredients for the ezme salad together in a large bowl, add the dressing and toss to combine. Transfer to a serving dish and scatter with the extra chopped parsley to garnish.

—— **How to serve**

This is excellent served with Tahini Sauce (see page 46) and flatbreads.

The Meal Before the Meal

Courgette Skewers
with Preserved Lemon & Hot Sauce

This recipe calls for a fermented hot sauce such as Cholula or sriracha. They all vary in heat, so start with the smallest amount first and see how you go, making these as hot or mild as you like. The seedy part of courgettes is too brittle to skewer, so keep those for something else, like a soup or stew. You will need eight 18cm (7-inch) wooden skewers.

Makes 8
—— **Vegan**

1kg (2lb 4oz) courgettes

For the preserved lemon & hot sauce marinade
½ tablespoon fennel seeds, lightly ground
3 garlic cloves, roughly chopped
50g (1¾oz) white miso
1–2¼ tablespoons hot sauce (see recipe introduction)
50g (1¾oz) preserved lemon, roughly chopped (for homemade, see page 18)
3 tablespoons agave syrup
¾ teaspoon fine sea salt
120ml (4fl oz) vegetable oil

Place your skewers in water to soak for at least 20 minutes before using.

Top and tail the courgettes, then shave them into long strips lengthways using a vegetable peeler. When you get to the seedy centres, stop and keep those for another occasion (or compost them).

Put the fennel seeds, garlic, miso, hot sauce, preserved lemon, agave syrup and salt in a jug and use a stick blender to blitz to a smooth paste. Slowly pour in the oil while continuing to blend until fully emulsified. If you don't have a stick blender, you can use a regular blender to blitz the solids before transferring to a bowl and slowly whisking in the oil until emulsified.

Preheat your grill to its hottest setting.

Thread the courgette strips on to the drained skewers, ribboning them on to create a concertina effect and leaving 2.5cm (1 inch) empty at either end. Transfer to a baking tray lined with foil, topping and tailing them to ensure they fit, and brush liberally all over with the marinade. Place under the grill and grill for 4–6 minutes, then turn with tongs and grill for a further 4–6 minutes on each of the 4 sides until they reach the same colour. Keep checking them, as some will colour quicker than others, so just turn the browned ones until they're golden on each side.

Transfer to a serving dish to serve.

Celeriac, Parmesan & Marmite Fritters

These are inspired by the iconic Parmesan fritters served at Brawn, a gorgeous neighbourhood restaurant in East London. The celeriac is quite subtle here; just a little earthiness against the cheese.

Serves 4-6 as a snack / Makes 18-20

500g (1lb 2oz) trimmed celeriac (about 1), peeled and chopped into 1cm (½-inch) cubes
400ml (14fl oz) whole milk, plus more if needed
1½ teaspoons fine sea salt
85g (3oz) unsalted butter, roughly cubed
1 teaspoon Marmite
100g (3½oz) plain flour
50g (1¾oz) Parmesan cheese, finely grated, plus more to serve
3 eggs
about 500ml (18fl oz) vegetable or sunflower oil, to deep-fry
sea salt flakes, to serve

Place the celeriac in a small saucepan along with the milk – the milk should just about cover the celeriac – then cover halfway with a lid. Bring up to a simmer, then reduce the heat to medium-low and simmer very gently for 35 minutes or until the celeriac is soft enough to mash. Reduce the heat if it begins to bubble over. Take off the heat and strain the celeriac through a sieve over a heatproof bowl. Return the celeriac to the saucepan along with 100ml (3½fl oz) of the cooking milk and blend into the smoothest purée you can with a stick blender.

Return the purée to the heat and gently cook out as much moisture as possible, stirring continuously for 6-8 minutes. Whisk in the salt, butter, Marmite, flour and Parmesan. Continue to whisk until everything is incorporated and the mixture is starting to come away from the sides of the pan, this should take a few minutes. You can tell it's ready when it starts to look glossy, is considerably thicker and balling up around the whisk. Turn off the heat and transfer to a large bowl, allowing to cool for around 10 minutes.

Once the mixture has cooled, crack in 1 egg at a time and whisk thoroughly to incorporate between each addition. At first, it will look like the mix has split, but if you keep whisking vigorously, it'll come together again.

Next, take a small saucepan and fill it about 7.5cm (3 inches) deep with oil. The oil must only come one-third of the way up the sides of the pan; any more than this and you might risk it bubbling over. Set the saucepan over a medium heat until it reaches 160°C (325°F). If you don't have a thermometer, a good way to tell if the oil is hot enough for frying is by taking a wooden spoon or chopstick and carefully placing its handle into the oil: if bubbles start to form around it, the oil is ready.

Dip 2 teaspoons in the oil, then take 1 heaped teaspoon of the mixture and drop this into the oil, using the other teaspoon to help push off the batter. Keep going: you can fry maybe 6 at a time, depending on the size of your pan (don't overcrowd it). Fry the fritters for 4-5 minutes or until golden, using a slotted spoon to flip them over halfway through. If they are browning too quickly, your oil is probably too hot, so reduce the heat, wait a little while, then begin again.

Transfer the fritters to a wire rack with a slotted spoon while you fry the rest.

Once they are cooled, sprinkle the fritters with sea salt flakes, then pile them on to your serving dish, grating over some more Parmesan.

How to serve

Offer a pile of these warm fritters to eat with drinks before a meal.

Ashkenazi Egg Mayonnaise

A friend recently coined the phrase 'high beige', which feels very apt in relation to this recipe, as this is top-tier beige food. Try to make it a day ahead so that the onions soften and meld with the egg. This recipe speaks so deeply to the Eastern European part of me, who grew up eating beige food and was comforted by its simplicity. Although this isn't literally a family recipe, it feels like a recipe inherited through generations: my great-great-grandparents could have eaten it as part of their shabbat table. And for this reason it gives a sense of homecoming. I don't know how it came to me; it just feels like it was always there.

Serves 4 as a small plate

200ml (7fl oz) neutral-flavoured oil
2 onions, halved and finely sliced
½ teaspoon fine sea salt, plus more to boil the eggs
6 eggs

For the mayonnaise
1 egg yolk
1 tablespoon Dijon mustard
1 teaspoon white wine vinegar
½ teaspoon freshly ground white pepper
½ teaspoon fine sea salt

—— **How to serve**

I like to eat this with challah bread or matzah crackers, or stuffed into very fluffy pitta breads with spears of spring onion for a bit of crunch.

Set a frying pan over a medium-low heat, add the onions and salt and sauté gently for 30 minutes until golden. Place a sieve over a heatproof bowl and strain them, then transfer the onions to a mixing bowl.

Cover the strained oil and place it in the fridge until completely cold, which will take around 2 hours. (If you use warm oil to make mayonnaise it will split, so this is very important!) If I'm in a rush, I like to put the oil in a food storage container and place it in the freezer for an hour.

Bring a saucepan of salted water to the boil. Boil the eggs for 8 minutes, then drain and plunge into cold water until cool. Shell the eggs and grate them on the coarse side of a grater, then add to the mixing bowl with the onions.

For the mayo, place a damp cloth under a small bowl to ensure it stays still while you whisk. Put the egg yolk in the bowl, add the mustard and vinegar and whisk together. Slowly whisk in the chilled oil in a steady stream until the mixture thickens and reaches a mayonnaise-like consistency. Season with the pepper and salt. If your mayonnaise splits, transfer it to a jug, clean and dry the bowl and tip in another egg yolk. Slowly whisk the split mixture into the egg yolk, as you did the oil, and it should come together again.

Add the mayonnaise to the eggs and onions, stir to combine, then either serve immediately, or (ideally) leave in the fridge overnight for the flavours to meld.

Caramelized Pomegranate Aubergine
with Lime Tahini

A delicious and substantial small plate, great as part of a dippy spread, but also a meal in itself. Its key influence came from the Sichuan dish 'sea-spice aubergine'. This is my Middle Eastern spin on it, with pomegranate molasses subbing for black vinegar. Both cuisines share the use of sesame paste, which is why tahini feels right. The celery provides a much-needed foil to the multilayered flavours. There's a lot going on... but in the best way.

Serves 4 as a small plate
—— **Vegan**

2 aubergines, cut into 1cm (½-inch) pieces
6 tablespoons olive oil
1 teaspoon fine sea salt
2 onions, halved lengthways and sliced into half moons
30g (1oz) coriander, roughly chopped, to serve

For the pomegranate sauce
3 garlic cloves, very finely chopped
1 tablespoon lightly crushed coriander seeds
½ tablespoon grated fresh root ginger
3 tablespoons pomegranate molasses
2 tablespoons agave syrup
1 tablespoon chilli crisp, plus 1 tablespoon to serve
1 tablespoon soy sauce
1 tablespoon rice vinegar
2 celery sticks, finely chopped

For the lime tahini
120g (4¼oz) tahini
finely grated zest and juice of 2 unwaxed limes (you need 50ml/2fl oz lime juice)
4 teaspoons agave syrup
½ teaspoon fine sea salt
3 tablespoons water

Preheat the oven to 180°C fan (400°F), Gas Mark 6. Line a baking tray with nonstick baking paper.

Set your aubergines on the lined baking tray, toss with 2 tablespoons of the oil and ½ teaspoon of the salt and roast for 30 minutes, tossing once halfway through, until golden and totally cooked through. Set aside.

Put the remaining 4 tablespoons of oil in a large frying pan and set over a medium heat. Add the onions and fry for about 10–15 minutes until golden and crisp. Add the aubergines along with the remaining ½ teaspoon of salt and cook for a further 2 minutes.

In a small bowl, mix together all the ingredients for the sauce except the celery until well combined. Pour the mixture into the onion pan, stir and cook for 2 minutes until it reduces and becomes sticky and glossy. Turn off the heat and leave to cook in the residual heat for 10 minutes or so before stirring in the celery.

Meanwhile, put all the ingredients for the lime tahini in a bowl and whisk together to combine.

Pour the lime tahini over a large serving dish and smooth it out, top with the aubergines and onions and scatter with the extra chilli crisp and the chopped coriander.

—— **How to serve**

Pair with lovely pitta bread and eggs, or fried tofu slices to make a full meal.

Sesame Chinese Leaf Skewers

A homage to one of my favourite restaurants in London, sadly now extinct, called Peg. It was perfect in every way, and I miss it deeply. I went there several times a month, and though not a vegetarian restaurant, their vegetarian dishes were some of the best I've eaten. I think about their cabbage salad – which inspired this recipe – regularly, as well as their chickpea tofu. If you ever went to Peg, or even if you didn't, I hope eating this puts a little smile on your face. You will need seven or eight 18cm (7-inch) wooden skewers.

Makes 7–8
—— **Vegan**

1 large head of Chinese leaf (about 850g/1lb 14oz)

For the sesame marinade
2 tablespoons white miso
4 tablespoons agave syrup
4 garlic cloves, peeled but left whole
4 tablespoons sesame oil
8 tablespoons toasted sesame seeds, plus more to serve
2 tablespoons rice vinegar
2 tablespoons mirin
6 tablespoons vegetable oil
2 teaspoons fine sea salt

Place your skewers in water to soak for at least 20 minutes before using.

Preheat your grill to its hottest setting.

Quarter the Chinese leaf from root to tip, then cut the quarters into 5cm (2-inch) pieces. Put them in a large mixing bowl.

Place all the marinade ingredients in a blender, ideally a high-powered bullet blender, and blitz into a smooth paste. Pour this over the Chinese leaf and stir (best to use your hands here) so that the marinade is coating the cabbage evenly.

Thread the cabbage evenly on all the drained skewers. Don't worry if some of the more leafy bits are a little floppy; the whole thing can be a little rustic and the contrast of crunchy stalk and crispy leaves makes these so much fun. Pack the cabbage tightly on the skewers to ensure it all cooks evenly, but leave 2.5cm (1 inch) empty at either end.

Transfer to a baking tray lined with foil and place under the grill for about 5 minutes on each side, turning once, until they are a little charred and caramelized. Once cooked, transfer to a serving plate and sprinkle with more sesame seeds to serve.

—— **How to serve**

These are, of course, very delicious skewers, but the recipe makes an equally delicious salad when you stop after you marinate the cabbage. One recipe, two glorious options: choose your own destiny.

The Meal Before the Meal

Pickled Aubergines & Tahini

My first chef job was at the mezze counter at The Palomar, a restaurant serving the food of Jerusalem in central London. These were my favourite – addictive fried vinegared aubergines – and I used to swallow slices whole while ducking down behind the bar during service. This is my homage to that dish, which stole my heart in my early days of cooking. This is for vinegar lovers only, as it's very tart and sharp, which is what makes it so moreish. You need to pickle the aubergine the day before for the flavours to meld, so all you have to do on the day is whip up the tahini.

Serves 4 as a small plate
—— *Vegan*

about 500ml (18fl oz) vegetable or sunflower oil, to deep-fry
2 large aubergines, stalk ends removed, sliced into 2.5cm (1-inch) rounds
1 jalapeño, halved, deseeded and finely sliced
30g (1oz) coriander, roughly chopped
200ml (7fl oz) white wine vinegar
2 tablespoons sweet smoked paprika
1 teaspoon chilli flakes
2 teaspoons fine sea salt
4 tablespoons lemon juice
4 garlic cloves, finely grated
1 teaspoon caster sugar
125ml (4fl oz) boiling water
Tahini Sauce (see page 46), to serve

Pour the oil into a saucepan. It must only come one-third up the sides of the pan; any more than this and you might risk the oil bubbling over. Set over a medium heat until the oil reaches about 180°C (350°F); if you don't have a thermometer, just heat it until the oil sizzles when an aubergine slice is added. Prepare a wire rack set over a baking tray alongside. Fry 4–5 aubergine slices at a time for about 5 minutes until golden brown and totally cooked through, flipping over for a further 5 minutes to colour on the other side. Once ready, transfer these to the wire rack. Repeat until all the aubergine is cooked.

Take a container with a lid, about 1-litre (1¾-pints) in capacity, and layer in the aubergine slices, sprinkling the jalapeño and half the roughly chopped coriander between each layer. Put the remaining ingredients in a bowl and whisk to combine thoroughly, then pour over the aubergines, ensuring they are totally covered. Place a sheet of nonstick baking paper over the top, cover with the lid and refrigerate until ready to use. (They will keep for up to 5 days.)

To serve, smooth the tahini sauce on to a serving dish. Drain the aubergine slices and lay them over the tahini, then garnish with the remaining coriander.

—— **How to serve**

While this is so good served as it is here on tahini sauce, pickled aubergine slices are also excellent with Labneh (see page 24) or Hummus (see pages 36–7), made into a little sandwich.

Wild Mushroom & Wakame Chilli Crisp
with Lime Ricotta

This is the love child of chilli crisp and sautéed mushrooms. I like to use robust mushrooms here, so I've opted for a mix of wild mushrooms. You can use whatever you can lay your hands on, but I'd make sure you have at least shiitake or oyster mushrooms in there, as they are excellent at soaking up flavour.

Makes 10 crostinis
—— **Can be made vegan**

250g (9oz) wild mushrooms (see recipe introduction), broken up into bite-sized pieces
toasted sourdough or baguette slices, to serve

For the lime ricotta
250g (9oz) ricotta cheese, or vegan alternative
finely grated zest of 2 unwaxed limes
⅛ teaspoon fine sea salt

For the wakame chilli crisp
100ml (3½fl oz) vegetable oil
100g (3½oz) shallots, halved lengthways, then sliced into thin strips lengthways
½ teaspoon fine sea salt
1 red chilli, halved lengthways and finely sliced
1 teaspoon grated fresh root ginger
3 garlic cloves, finely sliced
leaves from 3 rosemary sprigs
1 teaspoon hot smoked paprika
1 tablespoon black sesame seeds
1 teaspoon chilli flakes
1 tablespoon wakame, soaked and drained
2 tablespoons soy sauce
2 tablespoons agave syrup

To make the lime ricotta, stir everything together in a bowl and set aside.

For the chilli crisp, heat the oil in a small saucepan over a low heat, add the shallots and salt and sauté for 10 minutes until looking soft and very slightly starting to colour. Add the chilli, ginger, garlic and rosemary and cook for a further 3–4 minutes until the garlic is starting to colour on the edges.

Put the smoked paprika, black sesame, chilli flakes and wakame in a heatproof bowl and place a sieve over the top. Pour the oil over before transferring the shallot mixture in the sieve to a plate lined with kitchen paper to cool and crisp up for 15 minutes, then stir it back into the spiced oil. Stir the oil thoroughly, before seasoning with the soy and agave syrup.

Place a nonstick frying pan over a medium-high heat and add your mushrooms; it may seem weird to cook them without any oil, but you're about to rehydrate them with the chilli crisp, so have faith. Cook for 7–10 minutes, stirring regularly, until the mushrooms are softened and cooked through, with a little colour. Pour in the chilli crisp and fry for 1–2 minutes, stirring continuously now, to let the mushrooms hydrate in the oil and all the flavours to come together. Transfer to a bowl to cool slightly.

I like to serve the lime ricotta and mushrooms in separate bowls, with a pile of toasted sourdough or little crostini of toasted baguette. Spread the lime ricotta on the toasts and spoon the chilli crisp mushrooms on top.

—— **How to serve**

You can also use this where you would an ordinary chilli crisp, on fried eggs, beans, cheese on toast or, frankly, whatever to make a breakfast or lunch extra-special.

Leek, Miso & Mango Chutney Skewers

The joy of vegetable skewers comes from the bits that are jammy and a little caught, caramelized and crisp. What makes all skewers – meat or vegetable – delicious is the variety of textures from areas cooking slightly differently, where smaller bits are crispier than the rest. You will need eight or nine 18cm (7-inch) wooden skewers.

Makes 8–9
—— *Vegan*

1kg (2lb 4oz) leeks, tough green tops discarded, roots trimmed and cut into 2.5cm (1-inch) rounds
sea salt flakes
lime halves, to serve

For the miso & mango chutney marinade
3 garlic cloves, roughly chopped
50g (1¾oz) white miso
1 tablespoon agave syrup, or maple syrup
100g (3½oz) mango chutney
1 tablespoon white wine vinegar
70ml (2⅓fl oz) vegetable oil
½ teaspoon fine sea salt
1 teaspoon nigella seeds

Place your skewers in water to soak for at least 20 minutes before using. Soak your leeks in cold water for 10 minutes to get rid of any grit.

Bring a large saucepan of lightly salted water to the boil. Blanch your leeks for 3 minutes, then drain and allow to cool for 15 minutes. Some of the leek pieces may come apart during the process. This is totally normal and you can still use these pieces; just thread them in between the whole coins of leek to ensure they don't burn.

Thread the leeks on to your drained skewers, with the cut sides facing outwards, like a lollipop. You want about 5 rounds of leek for each skewer, depending on size, leaving 2.5cm (1 inch) empty at either end. Place them on a baking sheet lined with foil.

For the marinade, place all the ingredients except the nigella seeds in a small blender and blitz until fully combined and emulsified. Transfer to a small bowl and stir in the nigella seeds. Use a pastry brush to brush the marinade on to the skewers, ensuring they are all evenly covered.

Preheat your grill to its hottest setting. Grill the skewers for 15 minutes, turning once halfway through, until both sides are blistered and golden. Place on a serving dish and sprinkle with a pinch of sea salt flakes, then serve with the lime halves on the side.

Parsnip Chips
with Poppy Seed Honey

A great wintry canapé, these are quite addictive – something I never thought I'd say about parsnips. If you don't fancy deep-frying them, you can also roast the parsnips in the oven before drizzling them with the honey.

Serves 4 as a snack or small plate
—— **Can be made vegan**

For the poppy seed honey
150g (5½oz) honey, or agave syrup
2 tablespoons black sesame seeds, ground to a coarse powder
1 tablespoon poppy seeds
1 teaspoon urfa chilli flakes, or regular chilli flakes
1 teaspoon smoked chilli flakes, or regular chilli flakes
1 teaspoon sea salt flakes

For the parsnip chips
fine sea salt, to boil the parsnips
1kg (2lb 4oz) parsnips, peeled and sliced into 2cm (¾-inch) coins on the diagonal
about 500ml (18fl oz) vegetable or sunflower oil, to deep-fry
sea salt flakes
lemon quarters, to serve

Stir all the ingredients for the honey together in a bowl until well combined, then set aside. If you're using honey and it is cold and solidified, heat it either in a microwave or a saucepan until it becomes runny.

Bring a saucepan of salted water to the boil, add the parsnips and boil for 7 minutes or until cooked through and beginning to turn slightly smooshy (to ensure optimum crispness when fried). Drain into a colander and leave for a few minutes, then shake them gently so that the edges rough up, again to maximize their ability to crisp up in the oil. Leave to steam-dry until all the moisture evaporates.

Pour the oil for deep-frying into a saucepan. It must only come one-third up the sides of the pan; any more than this and you might risk the oil bubbling over. Heat to 180°C (350°F) or, if you don't have a thermometer, until it sizzles straight away when you drop in a parsnip chip. Use a slotted spoon to lower the parsnips into the hot oil, in batches of 4–5, and fry for 5–8 minutes until golden and crisp. Remove with the slotted spoon and transfer to a plate lined with kitchen paper, then sprinkle with sea salt flakes. Repeat to cook all the parsnips.

Once all the parsnips are fried, transfer to a serving dish, drizzle over the honey and serve with the lemon quarters on the side for people to squeeze over (hold back from doing this before serving or they'll turn soggy).

—— **How to serve**

The poppy seed honey here is a revelation. This recipe makes more than you need to drizzle on your parsnips, but it's a lovely thing to have in your larder for drizzling over fried halloumi or baked feta.

Sweetcorn Ribs, Black Garlic & Chipotle Butter

A reliable test of a recipe is how much of it I devoured when I made it, and the answer here is all of it... all four portions. Warning: deep-frying sweetcorn is not for the faint-hearted, as the kernels occasionally pop. There was a running joke at Bubala that whoever was on the fryer on a Saturday night, frying 20 portions at a time, was on a kamikaze mission. But this is worth it. Just make sure the saucepan is totally dry before adding oil, and *stand back* while the corn is frying. Also mandatory: eating this with your hands.

Serves 4 as a small plate
—— Can be made vegan

For the black garlic & chipotle butter
75g (2¾oz) unsalted butter, or vegan butter, very soft
1½ tablespoons tomato purée
1 teaspoon fine sea salt, plus more for the sweetcorn
1½ teaspoons black garlic paste
1½ teaspoons chipotle paste
3 tablespoons desiccated coconut, toasted
finely grated zest of 2 unwaxed limes, plus 50ml (2fl oz) lime juice
1½ tablespoons olive oil
1 teaspoon ground cumin

For the sweetcorn ribs
4 sweetcorn cobs, husks removed
about 500ml (18fl oz) vegetable or sunflower oil, to deep-fry

In a large bowl, whisk together all the ingredients for the butter until completely combined. Set aside.

Cut each corn cob in half horizontally, then each half into 4 lengthways through the core. This may be pretty tricky to do, so tap the back of the knife with your palm to help push the knife through.

Take a small saucepan, fill it about 5cm (2 inches) deep with oil and set over a medium heat. The oil must only come one-third up the sides of the pan; any more than this and you might risk the oil bubbling over. Heat the oil to 180°C (350°F) or, if you don't have a thermometer, until the oil sizzles when you drop in a kernel of corn.

Preheat the oven to 100°C fan (250°F), Gas Mark ½.

Deep-fry the corn in 2 batches for 5–7 minutes until the corn is golden. Remove with a slotted spoon and transfer to a baking tray lined with kitchen paper, sprinkle with a little salt, then place in the oven to keep warm while you fry the remaining corn.

Once you've fried all the corn, add it to the butter, stirring to ensure every piece of corn is entirely coated. Transfer to a serving dish.

Halloumi & Ricotta Fritters
with Spiced Lemon Syrup

Honestly, I didn't know what to call these: they're essentially very light patties of cheese in a crispy coating, not quite a croquette, not quite a fritter, absolutely not a nugget. They are a little fiddly to breadcrumb, so it definitely helps to chill the mix for an hour or so beforehand. The fritters are delicate and floral: it's the dip that pulls it all together, so I'm pretty insistent when serving these that everyone must double-dip. You can fry them slightly ahead of time and heat through in the oven just before serving.

Serves 10 as a snack / Makes about 20

For the spiced lemon syrup
50ml (2fl oz) lemon juice
100g (3½oz) agave syrup, or maple syrup
1 teaspoon ras el hanout (for homemade, see page 18)
⅛ teaspoon fine sea salt
1 small garlic clove, finely grated

For the fritters
225g (8oz) halloumi cheese, grated
500g (1lb 2oz) ricotta cheese
30 twists of black pepper
½ teaspoon baking powder
50g (1¾oz) plain flour
finely grated zest of 3 unwaxed lemons
10g (¼oz) oregano leaves, finely chopped, or thyme leaves, plus 1 tablespoon leaves to serve
½ teaspoon fine sea salt
about 500ml (18fl oz) vegetable or sunflower oil, to deep-fry
sea salt flakes, to serve

To crumb
150g (5½oz) panko crumbs
2 tablespoons sesame seeds
2 eggs, lightly beaten
70g (2½oz) plain flour
¼ teaspoon fine sea salt

Stir all the ingredients for the spiced lemon syrup together, transfer to a ramekin and set aside.

For the fritters, put all the ingredients, except for the oil and sea salt flakes, in a mixing bowl and stir thoroughly to combine.

Next you need to bread them, which can be a bit messy. Combine the panko and sesame seeds in a medium-sized bowl. Have the eggs ready in another, and the flour combined with the salt in a third bowl. With wet hands, weigh the mixture out into 30g (1oz) balls; you should have about 20. Gently toss them in the flour to coat, then lay them on a chopping board. Next, dip each into the eggs, allowing any excess to drip off, then coat thoroughly in the panko and sesame mixture. To prevent this getting too messy, keep one hand for the dry elements and the other for the eggs. Place the crumbed croquettes on a tray lined with nonstick baking paper.

To fry, place enough vegetable oil in a 28cm (11-inch) frying pan to come 1.5cm (⅝ inch) up the sides. Set over a medium high heat, then when it's hot, place half the fritters in the oil. Fry for 1–1½ minutes on each side until golden, using a slotted spoon and a regular spoon to help flip them over in the oil. Once cooked, place on a plate lined with kitchen paper to absorb any excess oil, then transfer to a serving dish. Scatter with the extra herbs, sprinkle with sea salt flakes and serve with the spiced lemon syrup for dipping.

Mushroom Skewers
with Tamari & Pomegranate

I was surprised to see fresh shiitake in my local small supermarket; they are a lot more robust than chestnut mushrooms, making them perfect to marinate and grill. Because they are deeply savoury, I wanted to add something to the marinade to cut through this, and pomegranate molasses makes such a good contrast. You will need eight 18cm (7-inch) wooden skewers.

Makes 8 skewers
—— **Vegan**

300g (10½oz) shiitake mushrooms
300g (10½oz) oyster mushrooms
sea salt flakes, to serve

For the tamari & pomegranate marinade
50ml (2fl oz) soy sauce, or tamari
60g (2¼oz) agave syrup, or maple syrup
45g (1¾oz) pomegranate molasses
100ml (3½fl oz) neutral-flavoured oil
2 garlic cloves, finely grated
1 tablespoon coriander seeds
1 teaspoon sweet smoked paprika

Place your skewers in water to soak for at least 20 minutes before using.

Combine all the ingredients for the marinade in a medium-sized mixing bowl and whisk together.

Take the large shiitake and halve them vertically through the stalk. The smaller shiitake can be left whole. With the oyster mushrooms, if they are in a clump, separate them into individual mushrooms. Large oyster mushrooms can be torn in half. Toss all the mushrooms into the marinade and coat thoroughly in the mix; you may want to go in with your hands (delicately) to ensure an even distribution. Leave to marinate for at least 30 minutes.

Preheat your grill to its hottest setting. Set a sieve over a saucepan and strain the mushrooms, reserving the marinade. To skewer the mushrooms, take a shiitake and skewer it through the middle, then an oyster mushroom. If the oyster mushroom is particularly long, you can fold it over itself and skewer it twice. Continue, leaving a 2.5cm (1-inch) length of skewer empty at either end, then transfer to a baking tray lined with foil. Repeat with the remaining 7 skewers.

Place the skewers under the grill for 10 minutes until they are nicely coloured, then remove them and flip them over using tongs. Return these to the grill for a further 8–10 minutes until they have reached the same colour on the other side.

Meanwhile, set the saucepan with the marinade over a medium heat and reduce for 5–6 minutes until thickened, then transfer to a bowl to cool. If the sauce is a little too thick, or looks like it has split, you can loosen it by whisking in a little water.

Transfer the skewers to your serving platter and drizzle over the reduced sauce. Finish with a pinch of sea salt flakes and serve.

Dill, Pea & Barberry Fritters
with Pomegranate Dip

I am calling these fritters, but honestly, the batter is almost invisible; it's essentially herbs and peas suspended in the lightest gossamer-like veil. They feel incredibly light and fresh, and I love the way they look so vibrant, losing none of their green colour during frying.

Serves 5 as a snack / Makes about 10
—— *Vegan*

1 red onion, halved lengthways and sliced into thin half moons
¾ teaspoon fine sea salt
30g (1oz) barberries
100g (3½oz) frozen peas, defrosted and drained
90g (3¼oz) coriander, roughly chopped
30g (1oz) dill, roughly chopped
50g (1¾oz) chickpea (gram) flour
65g (2½oz) cornflour
½ teaspoon baking powder
2 teaspoons cumin seeds
½ teaspoon ground turmeric
50ml (2fl oz) water
vegetable oil, to fry

For the pomegranate dip
1 tablespoon soy sauce, or tamari
1 tablespoon pomegranate molasses
1 teaspoon toasted sesame oil
½ tablespoon agave syrup
½ tablespoon water

Mix the red onion with the salt in a large mixing bowl and leave for 10 minutes or until a little liquid has seeped from the onion.

Meanwhile, put the barberries in a small heatproof bowl, cover with boiling water and leave for 10 minutes until plump, then drain thoroughly.

Mix the peas into the red onion bowl with the coriander, dill and drained barberries, then add the chickpea flour, cornflour, baking powder, cumin seeds and turmeric. Stir thoroughly so that it's all evenly distributed before stirring in the measured water. Stir thoroughly again; the mixture will still look quite dry, but the water is just enough to allow for the flours to cling to the vegetables.

Put all the ingredients for the dip in a small bowl and stir to combine before setting aside.

Take a large nonstick frying pan, cover the base with a 2.5cm (1-inch) depth of vegetable oil and set over a medium-high heat. You'll be able to make 3 fritters in each batch, to save overcrowding the pan. For each fritter, add 2 heaped tablespoons of the batter, pressing them down very lightly, being careful not to flatten entirely. Repeat twice more, leaving ample space between each to prevent them sticking together.

Fry for 1–1½ minutes until light golden before using a spatula or fish slice to flip them over. Fry on the other side for the same amount of time until equally golden, then transfer to a tray lined with kitchen paper. Repeat until you have fried all the mixture; you should have roughly 10 fritters.

Transfer to serving plates or a platter, with the dip alongside for drizzling.

—— **How to serve**

Of course, these are lovely as part of a mezze spread, but I also often make them for breakfast and serve them with a little yogurt and boiled eggs on the side.

Black Lime & Sichuan Pepper Courgette Fritti

This spice mix is crazy-addictive and quite unusual, owing to the combination of black lime and Sichuan pepper. To be honest, I would scale up the spice mix if you are going to the trouble of making it, saving it to dust on anything deep-fried, such as tempura, potato chips, crispy kale or sweet potato… it's a bit of magic.

Serves 4–6 as a snack
— *Vegan*

800g (1lb 12oz) courgettes
600ml (20fl oz) plant-based milk (or dairy milk)
1 litre (1¾ pints) vegetable oil, to deep-fry

For the flour mix
200g (7oz) plain flour
200g (7oz) cornflour
1 teaspoon fine sea salt

For the black lime & Sichuan pepper spice mix
1 teaspoon fine sea salt
1 teaspoon caster sugar
3 teaspoons MSG
5 black limes
1 star anise
1 teaspoon Sichuan pepper
1 teaspoon black peppercorns
1 tablespoon sumac
1 teaspoon cumin seeds

Top and tail your courgettes, then cut them in half horizontally. Slice them lengthways as finely as you can, around 5mm (¼-inch) wide. Pile up your slices and cut them lengthways again to the same width into fine matchsticks. Put these in a bowl or container and cover with the milk so that they're entirely submerged while you prepare the other bits.

Whisk the flour mix ingredients together in a large mixing bowl.

For the spice mix, put everything in a small, high-powered bullet blender and blitz to a fine powder. Transfer to a small dish.

Pour the oil into a saucepan. The oil must only come one-third up the sides of the pan; any more than this and you might risk the oil bubbling over. Heat to 180°C (350°F) or, if you don't have a thermometer, you can test the heat by seeing if a courgette piece sizzles as soon as you add it to the oil. Prepare a wire rack set over a baking tray alongside.

Drain your courgettes and, in batches, toss them in the flour mix, using your hands to move them about and making sure they're evenly covered. Place a sieve over another mixing bowl and, in batches, add a large handful of the courgette, shaking off the extra flour. Only do this just before you are going to fry them, to prevent them getting sticky.

Deep-fry the handful of courgette for 2–4 minutes until golden. Use a slotted spoon to transfer the fritti to the wire rack and sprinkle lightly with the spice mix. Keep frying until you've finished all the fritti, draining and spicing as you go. Transfer to a serving dish while still hot.

Spiced Farinata
with Radicchio & Feta

You'll want to be sure to allow at least an hour here for the chickpea mix to stand before using it so that it absorbs all the liquid, making for a much better texture. Do not skip the garam masala; it really pulls everything together.

Serves 16 as a canapé, or 4-6 as a starter or small plate / Makes 2
—— **Can be made vegan**

160g (5¾oz) chickpea (gram) flour
5 tablespoons olive oil, plus 4 tablespoons to fry the pancakes
250ml (9fl oz) water
1 teaspoon fine sea salt
2 teaspoons garam masala

For the radicchio & feta
4 tablespoons olive oil
1 teaspoon fine sea salt
2 tablespoons balsamic vinegar
finely grated zest of 1 unwaxed orange, plus 2 tablespoons orange juice
3 tablespoons agave syrup
1½ teaspoons chopped rosemary leaves
2 garlic cloves, finely grated
1½ tablespoons sumac
2 heads of radicchio (total weight about 500g/1lb 2oz), main stalks removed, cut into 5cm (2-inch) chunks
½ red onion, finely sliced
20g (¾oz) pine nuts, toasted
120g (4¼oz) feta cheese, or vegan alternative, roughly crumbled

Preheat the oven to 180°C fan (400°F), Gas Mark 6.

Whisk all the ingredients for the farinatas together in a bowl until totally smooth. Cover and set aside for at least 1 hour at room temperature.

For the radicchio, put the oil, salt, balsamic, orange juice, agave syrup, rosemary, garlic and sumac in a bowl and whisk to combine. Add the radicchio and toss to combine, ensuring all the pieces are covered, before transferring to a roasting tin. Roast for 15 minutes until wilted and caramelized in parts. Set aside.

Crank up the oven to 220°C fan (475°F), Gas Mark 9.

To cook the pancakes, set a heavy, oven-safe 29cm (11½-inch) frying pan over a high heat and pour in half the olive oil. Once the oil is shimmering, give the batter a quick stir to loosen it, then pour in half. Tilt and swirl the pan gently so that the batter spreads into an even layer. Let it sit on the heat for about 30 seconds, just until bubbles start to form on the surface. Then slide the pan into the hot oven and bake for 6–8 minutes or until the top is golden and just set in the centre. Lift the pancake out on to a plate and cover it with a clean tea towel to keep warm while you make the second pancake in the same way.

To serve, add the red onion, pine nuts and feta to the roasted radicchio and toss to combine. Cut the farinatas into 8 slices each and serve with the roasted radicchio.

—— **How to serve**

There are many options here. You can serve these cut small as a little canapé, with the pancakes cut into triangles and the roasted radicchio piled on top, or you can also have them for dinner with bigger slices of farinata; a perfect and complete meal that I love. Choose your own adventure but just be aware the farinatas are best eaten hot.

Beetroot, Black Garlic & Lime Leaf

This manages to feel both Eastern European and South East Asian simultaneously, a fusion I never knew I needed until it came to me one day when I was playing in the kitchen. Not being the world's number-one beetroot lover, I'd made it my mission to see if I could create a vibrant, surprising dressing to convert the beet sceptic, and here we are.

Serves 4 as a small plate
—— *Vegan*

500g (1lb 2oz) cooked beetroot, finely chopped into 5mm (¼-inch) pieces
200g (7oz) cherry tomatoes, finely chopped into 5mm (¼-inch) pieces
½ red onion, finely chopped
1 tablespoon finely chopped dill, plus dill fronds to serve
40g (1½oz) walnuts, toasted and roughly chopped

For the black garlic & lime leaf dressing
40g (1½oz) black garlic, peeled and roughly chopped
1 tablespoon rice vinegar
1 teaspoon fine sea salt
½ tablespoon date syrup
4 tablespoons neutral-flavoured oil
2 tablespoons lime juice
4 lime leaves, finely chopped
1 green bird eye chilli, roughly chopped

Make the dressing by putting all the ingredients in either a high-powered bullet blender or the small bowl of a regular blender and blitzing until completely smooth and homogenous. Set aside.

Put the beetroot, tomatoes, red onion and dill in a bowl and toss with the dressing. Transfer to a serving dish and scatter with the walnuts and dill fronds to serve.

—— **How to serve**

I love to include this in a mezze spread, as it's great scooped up with crackers or bread, but it also works well as a side salad.

Roast Watermelon, Silken Tofu & Crispy Onions

Roasting watermelon chunks gives them such an interesting texture and also means they soak up so much flavour, transforming into sweet-savoury flavour bombs. This is a very fresh, summery appetizer; just make sure your tofu is chilled for maximum refreshment.

Serves 3–4 as a small plate
—— *Vegan*

600g (1lb 5oz) watermelon, peeled and cut into 2cm (¾-inch) dice
1 tablespoon vegetable oil
1 tablespoon sesame oil
1½ tablespoons soy sauce, or tamari
2 teaspoons rice vinegar
1 tablespoon agave syrup, or maple syrup
½ teaspoon fine sea salt
1 teaspoon toasted sesame seeds
1½ tablespoons lime juice
½ tablespoon chilli crisp with sediment
15g (½oz) coriander, finely chopped
480g (1lb 1oz) silken tofu, drained
25g (1oz) crispy onions (shop-bought are fine here)

Preheat the oven to 180°C fan (400°F), Gas Mark 6.

Put the watermelon in a large bowl and toss with the oils, soy, rice vinegar, agave syrup and salt. Transfer to a roasting tray and cook for 45 minutes, tossing halfway through, until the watermelon chunks have much reduced in volume and are looking jammy and a deep red colour. It's a weird comparison to make in a vegetarian book, but they should look a bit like tuna. The liquid should have mostly reduced, leaving just the oils behind.

Allow to cool to room temperature before transferring to a bowl with about 2 tablespoons of the cooking liquid, then season with the sesame seeds, lime juice, chilli crisp and coriander.

Slice your tofu into 2cm (¾-inch) pieces and lay them on a serving platter so that they overlap each other. Sprinkle the roast watermelon over and scatter with the crispy onions to serve.

—— **How to serve**

You could serve this with some sticky rice and enjoy it as a main course, or serve it as part of a mezze spread.

Lime & Ras el Hanout Peppers
with Chive Ricotta

Some recipes take months to develop, others come together in a matter of minutes, often when you're thinking about something totally different. This was one of the latter. It's a great dish to get ahead on: you can marinate the peppers overnight and keep the chive ricotta in the fridge until ready to serve. Feel free to sub out the ras el hanout for smoked paprika, if you prefer.

Serves 4 as part of a mezze
—— **Can be made vegan**

6 large romano peppers
70g (2½oz) red chillies

For the lime & ras el hanout marinade
50ml (2fl oz) lime juice
1 tablespoon soy sauce
1 tablespoon olive oil
1½ tablespoons maple syrup, or agave syrup
½ teaspoon fine sea salt
½ teaspoon ras el hanout (for homemade, see page 18, or see recipe introduction)

For the chive ricotta
250g (9oz) ricotta cheese, or vegan alternative
15g (½oz) Parmesan cheese, or vegan alternative, finely grated
2 garlic cloves, finely grated
½ teaspoon fine sea salt
10g (¼oz) chives, finely chopped, plus 1 tablespoon to serve
finely grated zest of 1 unwaxed lime
1 teaspoon olive oil
good grind of black pepper

To serve
slices of toasted sourdough
50g (1¾oz) blanched hazelnuts, roasted and roughly chopped

Preheat your grill to its hottest setting. Line a baking tray with foil, add the peppers and chillies and place under the grill for 10 minutes on each side until blackened and blistered. Transfer to a bowl, cover with clingfilm and let them steam for 10 minutes, to help loosen the skins.

When the peppers are cool enough to handle, peel off their charred skins with your fingers or a small knife, then split open and remove the seeds, transferring the flesh to a bowl. Take the chillies and peel and deseed them in the same way, then slice into 2mm (¹/₁₆-inch) strips and add to the peppers. Add all the marinade ingredients, stir, cover and leave to marinate for at least 2 hours in the fridge.

Stir all the ingredients for the ricotta together in a bowl.

Assemble the ingredients on little sourdough toasts, spreading the ricotta on the bottom, topping with the peppers, sprinkling over the hazelnuts and finishing with the extra chopped chives.

Hoisin & Coriander Seed Celeriac Skewers

In preparation for a residency at a wine bar in London, I was searching for a snack that paired perfectly with a drink. I finally landed on this recipe, inspired by a char siu marinade, and it turned out to be the most-ordered dish. These are also delicious grilled on a barbecue; cooking them low and slow is key so that the celeriac cooks through by the time the marinade begins to caramelize. You will need eight 18cm (7-inch) wooden skewers.

Makes 8
—— *Vegan*

1 celeriac
sea salt flakes, to serve

For the hoisin & coriander seed marinade
100g (3½oz) maple syrup, or agave syrup
2½ tablespoons red miso
2½ tablespoons hoisin sauce
1½ tablespoons soy sauce
3 garlic cloves, finely grated
1 tablespoon coriander seeds
125ml (4fl oz) rapeseed oil

Place your skewers in water to soak for at least 20 minutes before using. Meanwhile, put all the ingredients for the marinade except the oil in a bowl and whisk to combine, then slowly whisk in the oil.

Cut the top and root off the celeriac and discard, then wash thoroughly. Cut into quarters, then use a mandoline to slice lengthways very finely. Put the celeriac slices in a mixing bowl, add half the marinade and toss to coat.

To assemble the skewers, thread the end of a celeriac slice on to a skewer, then loop the rest of the slice back and forth to create a concertina effect as you thread it all on. Repeat until you have threaded an equal quantity of the celeriac slices on to each skewer, leaving 2.5cm (1 inch) empty at either end.

Preheat your grill to its hottest setting. Lay the skewers on a large baking tray lined with foil and place under the grill for about 10 minutes on each side, removing every few minutes to turn and brush with the remaining marinade, until the celeriac is golden and a little charred. Brush once more with the marinade, then transfer to a serving plate and sprinkle with sea salt flakes to serve.

The Main Event

Tamarind Pumpkin, Confit Garlic & Orzo

When choosing a pumpkin, Delica or Violina varieties have extra-sweet flesh, which works so well with sharp tamarind. However, this is also good with butternut squash. It's fun to cook (well, certainly my idea of fun), as you make an infused oil that is used in two different ways: first to make a dressing, then to toast the orzo.

Serves 4
—— **Vegan**

1kg (2lb 4oz) pumpkin (see recipe introduction), deseeded and cut into 5cm (2-inch) wedges
1 tablespoon olive oil
½ teaspoon fine sea salt
good grind of black pepper

For the confit garlic oil
1 garlic bulb, cloves separated and peeled
100ml (3½fl oz) olive oil, plus more if needed
10g (¼oz) rosemary leaves
⅛ teaspoon fine sea salt
1 red chilli, halved lengthways

For the orzo
300g (10½oz) orzo
½ teaspoon fine sea salt
750ml (1⅓ pints) hot vegetable stock

For the tamarind dressing
3 teaspoons tamarind paste
1½ tablespoons date syrup
1 tablespoon soy sauce
⅛ teaspoon fine sea salt
2 tablespoons lime juice

For the confit garlic oil, place the garlic cloves, oil, rosemary, salt and red chilli in the smallest saucepan you have and set over a low heat. Ideally you want the garlic as submerged as possible to ensure it cooks evenly, so add a little more oil if needed (you can save any excess for future cooking). Simmer as gently as possible until the garlic is soft and can be crushed with the back of a spoon; this takes around 20 minutes, but stir it occasionally to prevent it catching. Once the confit garlic is done, strain out the aromatics through a sieve set over a bowl and transfer the crispy rosemary and garlic cloves to a plate lined with kitchen paper to cool, reserving the oil.

Preheat the oven to 180°C fan (400°F), Gas Mark 6. Line a baking dish with nonstick baking paper.

Place the pumpkin in the lined dish and toss in the olive oil, salt and pepper. Roast for 35–40 minutes until completely cooked through and beginning to colour.

Meanwhile, transfer 4 tablespoons of the garlic oil to a small bowl to make the dressing, then pour the rest into a saucepan set over a medium heat. Stir in the orzo and salt and toast for 2 minutes until the orzo smells nutty. Add the hot stock and bring to the boil, then reduce the heat to low. Let the orzo cook, uncovered, for 10–12 minutes, stirring regularly, until the liquid is mostly absorbed and the orzo is cooked through.

Now for the dressing. To the 4 tablespoons of reserved garlic oil, add all the dressing ingredients and whisk until fully combined.

Transfer the cooked orzo to a serving dish and top with the pumpkin, ensuring the wedges are spread out across the plate. Drizzle over your tamarind dressing, then scatter with the crispy rosemary and confit garlic cloves.

Kohlrabi & Nori Crème Fraîche
with Pistachio Salsa

Kohlrabi tastes to me like a deeply savoury, turnipy apple, a flavour that intensifies when you roast it. Because of this clean salinity, I pair it with nori and wasabi, both of which remind me of the sea. When it is roasted, kohlrabi is soft and fudgy with a little sweetness where it caramelizes. Just be sure to remove the stringy bits under the tough outer skin when peeling, which is best done with a pairing knife.

Serves 4

1–1.2kg (2lb 4oz–2lb 11oz) kohlrabi, peeled (see recipe introduction)
3 tablespoons olive oil
½ teaspoon fine sea salt

For the nori crème fraîche
1 sheet of nori, blitzed into a fine powder
300ml (10fl oz) crème fraîche
½ teaspoon fine sea salt
finely grated zest of 1 unwaxed lime
1 garlic clove, finely grated
¼ teaspoon wasabi paste (optional)

For the pistachio salsa
45g (1½oz) shelled unsalted pistachios, lightly toasted
4 tablespoons olive oil
2 tablespoons lime juice
6 teaspoons agave syrup
1 teaspoon fine sea salt
1 teaspoon sumac
1 teaspoon rice vinegar
15g (½oz) mint leaves, finely chopped

Preheat the oven to 180°C fan (400°F), Gas Mark 6.

Cut each kohlrabi into 8–10 wedges, depending on size, and toss with the olive oil and salt on a baking tray. Roast for 30 minutes, tossing halfway through, until golden and caramelized.

Meanwhile, stir together all the ingredients for the nori crème fraîche in a bowl.

For the salsa, put the pistachios in a blender and pulse-blend a few times until you have a coarse rubble, with chunkier and more powdery bits. Tip into a small bowl and stir in the rest of the salsa ingredients.

To serve, spread the nori crème fraîche on to a serving dish, top with the roasted kohlrabi and sprinkle over the pistachio salsa.

Courgettes, Peanut Tahini & Pickled Fennel

Cooking the fennel in a dry pan before adding the lime is a cool technique, as it both cooks and pickles the fennel at the same time. I like to use the Mexican Gran Luchito brand of jalapeños that chars the chillies before pickling, but any kind works nicely here. Both the tahini and fennel can be made ahead; just make sure they're not fridge cold when you serve.

Serves 6
— **Vegan**

750g (1lb 10oz) courgettes, halved vertically, then halved horizontally
½ teaspoon fine sea salt
2 tablespoons olive oil

For the pickled fennel
1 fennel bulb, tops, tough outer leaves and core removed, finely chopped (about 200g/7oz)
2 tablespoons lime juice
6 lime leaves, roughly chopped
75ml (2½fl oz) olive oil
1 tablespoon pickled jalapeño brine
60g (2¼oz) pickled jalapeños, finely chopped
½ teaspoon fine sea salt

For the peanut tahini
1 tablespoon agave syrup
1½ teaspoons white miso
150g (5½oz) tahini
½ teaspoon fine sea salt
2½ tablespoons smooth peanut butter
2 tablespoons lime juice
75ml (2½fl oz) water

For the fennel, take a nonstick saucepan and set it over a high heat. Add the fennel and cook, without any oil, for 4–5 minutes until charred, tossing regularly to ensure it colours evenly. Add the lime juice and stir for a further 30 seconds until it's all absorbed and the fennel is looking slightly sticky. Transfer to a bowl.

If you have a high-powered bullet blender, use it to blend the lime leaves and oil together until it feels hot to the touch (or reaches 85°C/185°F if you have a probe thermometer); this will take about 3 minutes. You can also do this in the small bowl of a regular blender: just blitz until the lime leaves are finely chopped and the colour of the oil has darkened a little to pale green. Strain this into the fennel along with the jalapeño brine, pickled jalapeños and salt, then set aside.

Put all the ingredients for the peanut tahini except the measured water in a small bowl and whisk to combine, then slowly add the water as you whisk until you have a sauce the consistency of thick pancake batter. You want it to be a bit thicker than regular tahini sauce, as the fennel mixture will cause it to thin a little when the dish is served.

To cook the courgettes, lay them cut side up and sprinkle with the salt. Leave for 5 minutes, then pat dry and heat the oil in a large nonstick frying pan over a high heat. Place the courgettes in the pan cut sides down and fry for 8–10 minutes until deeply browned. Flip over and cook for a further 2 minutes. This will give you quite an al dente courgette, but by all means cook them further if you wish them to be softer.

Smooth the tahini over a serving plate, then top with the courgettes and fennel.

The Main Event

Celeriac & Curried Burnt Butter

A very rich, nutty sauce here complements celeriac's deep savouriness. It's an absolute must to serve this with rice, and I recommend my Magic Rice (see page 150). You can use vegan butter, though it won't caramelize in the same way; you can just melt it before adding the spice paste, or use olive oil instead.

Serves 4
—— *Can be made vegan*

2 celeriac (about 600g/1lb 5oz each), trimmed, peeled and each cut into 8 wedges
4 tablespoons olive oil
1 teaspoon fine sea salt
good grind of black pepper
80g (2¾oz) pea shoots, to serve

For the curry paste
6 lime leaves, roughly chopped
80g (2¾oz) shallots, roughly chopped
3 garlic cloves, roughly chopped
1 black lime, finely ground (optional)
4 tablespoons water
1 tablespoon garam masala
2 tablespoons tomato purée
2 teaspoons fine sea salt
2 tablespoons agave syrup, or maple syrup
1 tablespoon vegan fish sauce
1 teaspoon chilli powder

For the burnt butter sauce
50g (1¾oz) unsalted butter, or vegan alternative (see recipe introduction)
250g (9oz) cherry tomatoes
400ml (14fl oz) can of coconut milk
400ml (14fl oz) hot vegetable stock
2 tablespoons lime juice

Preheat the oven to 180°C fan (400°F), Gas Mark 6. Line a baking tray with nonstick baking paper.

Place the celeriac wedges on the lined tray and toss with the oil, salt and pepper. Roast for 35 minutes, turning halfway through. Once cooked and nicely coloured, set aside.

For the curry paste, put all the ingredients in a blender, ideally a high-powered bullet blender, and blitz until totally smooth.

For the sauce, set a nonstick pan over a medium heat. Add the butter and allow to melt; regular dairy butter will gently start to foam, which will take around 3 minutes. Swirl the butter gently around the pan and allow it to continue bubbling and foaming. It's important to pay very close attention, as it can go from brown to burnt very quickly! The butter will begin to smell nutty, and you'll notice brown solids at the bottom of the pan: these are caramelized milk solids, and a sign that your butter is ready. At this point, add the curry paste; careful, as it will splutter. Stir thoroughly and cook for 2–3 minutes until the paste smells aromatic.

Now add the cherry tomatoes, coconut milk and hot stock, stir thoroughly to combine and simmer gently for about 30–40 minutes or until the tomatoes are slightly collapsed and jammy and the sauce is thickened and almost halved in volume. Turn off the heat and stir in the lime juice.

Toss the roasted celeriac wedges in the sauce so that everything is hot. Spoon on to a serving dish, pour over the remaining sauce and scatter with the pea shoots to serve.

Marzipan Cauliflower
with Caraway Oil

Believe it or not, this idea came to me in a dream. There is an almondy quality to cauliflower, so I thought it would be fun to envelop it in ground almonds; it sort of melts together. But that's where the marzipan similarities end. Make the *ajo blanco* and caraway oil ahead, stirring the mint through the oil just before serving.

Serves 4

—— **Can be made vegan**

1 large cauliflower
250g (9oz) Greek yogurt, or vegan alternative
½ teaspoon fine sea salt
2 tablespoons olive oil, plus more to cook
50g (1¾oz) ground almonds
2 garlic cloves, finely grated
½ teaspoon almond extract (optional)

For the caraway oil
65ml (2¼fl oz) olive oil
4 star anise
1 cinnamon stick
1 tablespoon caraway seeds
5 cloves
1 tablespoon fennel seeds
1 tablespoon Aleppo chilli flakes
¼ teaspoon fine sea salt
½ tablespoon agave syrup
1 tablespoon lemon juice
50g (1¾oz) blanched almonds, toasted and roughly chopped
15g (½oz) mint leaves, roughly torn

For the ajo blanco
60g (2¼oz) ground almonds
5½ tablespoons water
1 garlic clove, finely grated
2 teaspoons sherry vinegar
50ml (2fl oz) olive oil
1 tablespoon lemon juice
½ teaspoon fine sea salt

Preheat the oven to 200°C fan (425°F), Gas Mark 7. Line a roasting tin with nonstick baking paper.

Break the cauliflower into florets and separate the leaves. Put the yogurt in a large bowl with the salt, olive oil, ground almonds, garlic and almond extract, if using, and whisk to combine. Add the cauliflower florets and leaves and toss thoroughly to coat before transferring them to the lined tin, ensuring it's all in a single layer. Sprinkle over a little more oil and roast for 35 minutes, turning the florets halfway through, until evenly golden in colour.

For the caraway oil, put the oil, star anise, cinnamon stick, caraway seeds, cloves and fennel seeds in a small saucepan and bring to a very gentle simmer (not to the boil). Simmer for 5 minutes or until the spices are aromatic. Turn off the heat and let the oil cool. Put the Aleppo chilli in a small bowl with the salt, syrup and lemon juice, setting a sieve over the top, then strain over the infused oil and discard the spices. Once the oil is completely cold, add the chopped almonds. Add the mint only just before serving so that it doesn't wilt.

For the ajo blanco, put the almonds, measured water, garlic and sherry vinegar in a jug and use a stick blender to blitz it into a smooth paste. With the blender still running, slowly trickle in the olive oil in a steady stream until thoroughly combined and you have a thick, emulsified sauce. Add the lemon juice and salt and briefly blitz to incorporate.

Spoon the ajo blanco over a serving dish and top with the cauliflower. Add the mint to the caraway oil, stir, then spoon it over to serve.

Lemongrass Parsnips
with Curry Leaves

Sometimes dishes come together quite magically and this was one of those ah-ha! moments when I was playing around with parsnips over Christmas, wanting to create something vibrant. The combination of rosemary and lemongrass melds the familiar with the new, which is why this is so fun to eat. Both the glaze and temper can be made ahead of time. I like to keep the parsnip skin on for texture, but feel free to peel if you prefer.

Serves 4
—— *Vegan*

1kg (2lb 4oz) parsnips
2 tablespoons olive oil
½ teaspoon fine sea salt
good grind of black pepper

For the lemongrass & rosemary glaze
6 lemongrass stalks
4 tablespoons olive oil
3 garlic cloves, chopped
2 teaspoons tamarind paste
2 teaspoons date syrup
1 teaspoon white miso (red miso also works)
1 teaspoon fine sea salt
leaves from 4 rosemary sprigs

For the curry leaf temper
4 tablespoons desiccated coconut
2 tablespoons yellow mustard seeds
30 fresh curry leaves
6 tablespoons vegetable oil
juice of 2 limes
¼ teaspoon fine sea salt

—— **How to serve**
The parsnips pack so much flavour that all they need alongside is plain rice and a crunchy salad.

Preheat the oven to 180°C fan (400°F), Gas Mark 6. Line 2 baking trays with nonstick baking paper.

Wash your parsnips thoroughly, then slice off the tops and cut each lengthways into quarters. Transfer to the lined trays and toss with the olive oil, salt and pepper. Roast the parsnips for 30 minutes, tossing halfway through, until golden.

Meanwhile, prepare your glaze. Top and tail the lemongrass and remove the woody outer layers until you are left with the pale and tender centres. Roughly chop, then add to a blender, ideally a high-powered bullet blender, with the remaining glaze ingredients and blend to a smooth paste (add a little water if you are having trouble blending the mixture).

For the temper, mix together the coconut, mustard seeds and curry leaves in a bowl; this cooks very quickly, so it's helpful to have everything ready and to keep the emptied bowl to hand. Heat the oil in a saucepan over a medium-high heat. Once hot, add the coconut mixture and fry, using a spatula to keep it moving, for 30–60 seconds until the curry leaves and mustard seeds pop and the coconut begins to darken. The mixture will continue cooking once removed from the pan due to the hot oil, so err on the side of caution here. Return the mix to the bowl and season with the lime juice and salt.

Once the parsnips are done, remove them from the oven and crank up the oven temperature to 220°C fan (475°F), Gas Mark 9. Pour the glaze over the parsnips and toss to coat, then roast for a further 5 minutes until sticky and golden. Transfer to a serving dish and pour over the curry leaf temper.

The Main Event —— 103

Leeks, Oregano Butter, Za'atar Feta

Just like my other buttery sauces, you want to keep the oregano butter in this one warm until you're ready to serve; you can always reheat it for a minute or two if it sets a little. If you can't track down fresh oregano, thyme is a great substitute.

Serves 4
—— *Can be made vegan*

1kg (2lb 4oz) leeks
3 tablespoons olive oil
½ teaspoon fine sea salt
good grind of black pepper
200ml (7fl oz) vegetable stock

For the za'atar feta
100g (3½oz) feta cheese, or vegan alternative, finely crumbled
1 teaspoon sumac
1 teaspoon za'atar
1 tablespoon olive oil
¼ teaspoon chilli flakes

For the oregano butter
100g (3½oz) unsalted butter, or vegan alternative
2 tablespoons oregano leaves (about 8g/¼oz) (or see recipe introduction)
2 garlic cloves, finely grated
1 teaspoon fine sea salt
70ml (2⅓fl oz) lemon juice

Preheat the oven to 180°C fan (400°F), Gas Mark 6. Line a baking tray with nonstick baking paper.

Trim the roots, tough green tops and outer leaves from the leeks and cut them in 3 horizontally, before cutting these lengths in half vertically. Soak these in cold water for 10 minutes to get rid of any grit.

Drain, then lay them out on the lined tray, season with the oil, salt and pepper. Pour in the stock, then cover tightly with foil and roast for 25–30 minutes until soft and cooked through.

Meanwhile, place all the ingredients for the za'atar feta in a small bowl and stir to combine. Set aside.

For the oregano butter, put the butter in a small saucepan, add the oregano, garlic and salt and simmer for 3–4 minutes until bubbling but not beginning to colour. Reduce the heat to low, then slowly whisk in the lemon juice; the mixture should emulsify and form a pale yellow sauce. Set aside. If it has solidified by the time you come to serve the dish, gently warm it through to a spoonable consistency.

Transfer the leeks to a serving dish: I like to lay them all in a line cut side up so that the sauce permeates them. Pour on the warm butter, then sprinkle over the za'atar feta.

—— **How to serve**

This works really nicely with the Lime Pickle & Miso Roasted Sweet Potato (see page 156).

Pilpil-style Roast Cabbage
with Shiitake & Preserved Lemon

The word *pilpil* actually refers to a Basque sauce for fish in which oil and garlic come together with the cooking juices, emulsifying into a thick sauce. The sauce is named *pilpil* after the way it sputters in the pan. This is my homage to that sauce, with the addition of preserved lemon.

Serves 4
—— **Vegan**

2 hispi or sweetheart cabbages, tough outer leaves removed

For the shiitake marinade
20g (¾oz) dried shiitake mushrooms, ground to a fine powder
130ml (4fl oz) olive oil, plus more if needed
1½ teaspoons fine sea salt
4 tablespoons date syrup
1 tablespoon white miso

For the pilpil sauce
4 garlic cloves, roughly chopped
4 tablespoons lemon juice
60g (2¼oz) preserved lemon, roughly chopped (for homemade, see page 18)
1 tablespoon agave syrup
¼ teaspoon fine sea salt
90ml (6 tablespoons) olive oil

For the spiced parsley
30g (1oz) parsley, finely chopped
1 teaspoon hot smoked paprika
2 teaspoons olive oil
⅛ teaspoon salt

Preheat the oven to 180°C fan (400°F), Gas Mark 6. Line a baking tray with nonstick baking paper.

Place all the ingredients for the shiitake marinade in a bowl and whisk until thoroughly combined; it will form a stiff paste.

Cut the cabbages in half through the cores and place on the lined tray. Spoon one-quarter of the marinade on the cut side of each cabbage and use the back of the spoon to press it into all the crevices, ensuring the cut side is evenly covered. If any areas look a little dry, give them a drizzle of olive oil. Roast for 30–35 minutes until the marinade is starting to look caramelized and you can slide a knife easily through the cores.

Meanwhile, for the sauce, place all the ingredients except the oil in a jug and use a stick blender to blitz it into a fine paste. With the blender still on, slowly add the olive oil, a trickle at a time, until it's all combined and you have a thickened, pale yellow sauce.

Make the spiced parsley by stirring all the ingredients together in a small bowl.

Smooth the pilpil sauce on to a serving dish, top with the warm cabbage halves and sprinkle over the spiced parsley to serve.

—— **How to serve**

This dish packs a punch with the sweet and umami marinade on the cabbage and the intensely lemony garlic sauce underneath. So it calls for some simplicity on the side in the form of Magic Rice, perhaps with Peas, Walnuts & Orange Blossom Water (see pages 150 and 180).

Carrots, Lime Tahini & Pumpkin Seed Salsa Macha

Probably one of the easiest dishes to put together in this book, with two sauces that just need to be stirred together ahead of time. In fact, you can make both the lime tahini and pumpkin seed salsa macha the day before and store them in the fridge, making this a near-effortless recipe for entertaining.

Serves 4
— *Vegan*

1kg (2lb 4oz) carrots, peeled but left whole (unless they're absolutely massive, when they can be halved lengthways)
2 tablespoons olive oil
½ teaspoon fine sea salt
good grind of black pepper

For the pumpkin seed salsa macha
4 tablespoons pumpkin seeds
1 tablespoon toasted sesame seeds
1 tablespoon harissa
6 tablespoons olive oil
¼ teaspoon fine sea salt
¼ teaspoon ground cumin

For the lime tahini
150g (5½oz) tahini
4 tablespoons lime juice
½ tablespoon agave syrup
1 teaspoon white miso
1 teaspoon soy sauce, or tamari
2½ tablespoons water, plus more if needed

Preheat the oven to 200°C fan (425°F), Gas Mark 7. Line a roasting tray with nonstick baking paper.

Place your carrots on the lined tray and add the olive oil, salt and pepper. Mix this all together, then roast for 25–30 minutes, turning halfway through. The idea is that these are cooked at a high temperature, to maintain some bite, but so they also become nicely burnished.

For the salsa macha, set a pan over a medium heat and add your pumpkin seeds. Toast for 3–4 minutes until the seeds pop and turn golden. You'll need to shake the pan regularly to ensure they colour evenly. Tip them into a blender and pulse very briefly until they resemble a coarse rubble. Transfer to a mixing bowl and stir in the remaining salsa macha ingredients.

For the tahini, put all the ingredients except the water in a mixing bowl and whisk to combine. Slowly pour in the measured water while whisking. You want the tahini sauce to be the same consistency as thick hummus, so you might want to add a little extra water if it's too thick.

To serve, smooth the tahini on to a serving dish, place your carrots on top and then drizzle over the salsa.

— **How to serve**
This would be especially lovely alongside Toasted Buckwheat Tabbouleh (see page 153).

The Main Event — 109

Roast Broccoli & Curried Sweetcorn Polenta
with Jalapeño Oil

I love making polenta from sweetcorn when I'm in the mood for something lighter than the regular variety. I also love old-fashioned broccoli, which is neglected in the face of the rise of its more bougie cousin, Tenderstem. Roasting broccoli makes the most of it; just peel off as much tough skin from the stem as possible, or it gets chewy after roasting. There's a triple threat of heat here: curry powder, jalapeño oil and chilli crunch, all adding different layers of spice and heat.

Serves 4
—— **Can be made vegan**

2 large heads of broccoli, stalks peeled, each cut into 4 through the stalk
6 tablespoons olive oil
½ teaspoon fine sea salt

For the curried sweetcorn polenta
6 sweetcorn cobs, husks removed, kernels shaved off with a sharp knife
1½ teaspoons fine sea salt
600ml (20fl oz) boiling water
60g (2¼oz) butter, or vegan alternative, cold and chopped
2 teaspoons hot curry powder

For the jalapeño oil
1 jalapeño, deseeded and roughly chopped
50ml (2fl oz) lime juice
3 tablespoons olive oil
¼ teaspoon fine sea salt

To serve
2 tablespoons chilli crisp oil with sediment
100g (3½oz) Greek yogurt, or vegan alternative

Preheat the oven to 180°C fan (400°F), Gas Mark 6. Line a large baking tray with nonstick baking paper.

Start with the polenta. Put the sweetcorn and salt in a saucepan and cover with the measured boiling water. Return to the boil, then cook for 5 minutes. Take off the heat and use a stick blender to blend until as smooth as possible. Place the blended corn over a low heat, add the butter and curry powder and stir regularly for 5–6 minutes until it's bubbling and looks slightly thickened. Careful: it will sputter.

Put the broccoli on the lined tray along with the olive oil and salt. Toss thoroughly to ensure it's all covered, paying special attention to the florets and making sure they are all oiled so that they crisp nicely. Roast for 25–30 minutes until a little charred and you can easily insert a knife through the thickest part of the stalks.

For the oil, put all the ingredients in a blender, ideally a high-powered bullet blender, and blitz until smooth.

To serve, spoon the polenta into a serving dish, top with the broccoli, drizzle over the oil and the chilli crisp and serve with the yogurt spooned on the side.

Flash-fried Mangetout
with Hazelnuts & Polenta

When summer hits and vegetables get smaller and crisper, I think they tend to start taking a bit of a backseat, relegated to the side salad arena. I don't think this needs to be the case, so this is a celebratory, substantial way to eat possibly my favourite summer vegetable. You can sub ground ancho chilli if you can't find guajillo. This recipe also works well with green beans in place of the mangetout.

Serves 4
—— *Can be made vegan*

finely grated zest of 1 unwaxed lemon, plus 2 tablespoons lemon juice
2 garlic cloves, finely chopped
leaves from 25g (1oz) basil, torn
2 tablespoons olive oil
450g (1lb) trimmed mangetout
1½ teaspoons fine sea salt

For the hazelnut salsa
50ml (2fl oz) olive oil
50g (1¾oz) blanched hazelnuts, toasted and roughly chopped
½ teaspoon guajillo chilli flakes (or see recipe introduction)
1 tablespoon toasted sesame seeds
½ teaspoon ground cinnamon
½ tablespoon soy sauce
1 tablespoon maple syrup
½ teaspoon fine sea salt

For the polenta
1.2 litres (2 pints) vegetable stock
2 teaspoons fine sea salt
230g (8oz) quick-cook polenta
50g (1¾oz) unsalted butter, or vegan alternative
30g (1oz) Parmesan cheese, or vegan alternative, finely grated

To make the salsa, place the olive oil in a small saucepan and heat until smoking, then turn off and leave to cool for 5 minutes. Or, if you have a food thermometer, heat the oil to 180°C (350°F). Place the remaining ingredients in a small heatproof bowl and pour over the oil. Mix to combine and set aside.

To make the polenta, bring the stock to the boil in a medium saucepan. Add the salt, then gradually pour in the polenta, whisking continuously to avoid lumps. Reduce the heat and continue whisking for 3–4 minutes until the polenta thickens and the whisk leaves tracks. Stir in the butter and Parmesan and check for seasoning, then turn off the heat and leave, covered, until ready to serve. You may want to add a little water to loosen it to your desired consistency if it firms up before you're ready.

Put the lemon zest and juice, garlic and basil in a heatproof bowl and stir to combine. Add the olive oil to a frying pan and set over a medium-high heat. Once smoking, add the mangetout and salt and cook for 3 minutes, tossing regularly, until the mangetout have softened and blistered in places. Add straight to the bowl with the lemon mix and toss to combine.

Spoon the polenta on to a serving dish and top with the flash-fried mangetout. Spoon over the hazelnut salsa and serve.

Hispi Cabbage, Date Butter & Tahini

The key here is to keep the spiced date butter warm, pouring it over the cabbages just before you take the dish to the table. If you have a barbecue going, finish the cabbages off on the grill for some lovely smokiness. A note on vegan butter: it won't caramelize, so just melt it before adding the dates, or use olive oil instead.

Serves 4
— **Can be made vegan**

2 hispi or sweetheart cabbages, tough outer leaves removed
4 tablespoons olive oil
½ teaspoon fine sea salt
good grind of black pepper

For the date butter
125g (4½oz) unsalted butter, or vegan alternative
150g (5½oz) pitted medjool dates, roughly chopped
3 teaspoons olive oil
1 tablespoon hawaij (for homemade, see page 19)
2 tablespoons lemon juice
½ tablespoon sherry vinegar
½ teaspoon fine sea salt

To serve
1 quantity Tahini Sauce (see page 46)
15g (½oz) coriander sprigs
1 teaspoon Aleppo chilli flakes

— **How to serve**

I love to serve this with Magic Rice (see page 150) or flatbreads, along with a fresh and crisp green salad with lemon and olive oil. I would add that this date butter is something special, so if you know what's good for you, I'd make double, blend the second batch to a smooth paste and save it for spreading on toast. I also love it in cheese toasties: hawaij and date pair so well with melted cheese.

Preheat the oven to 180°C fan (400°F), Gas Mark 6. Line a baking tray with nonstick baking paper.

Cut the cabbages in half through the cores and season with the oil, salt and pepper. Place on the lined tray and roast for 35 minutes until thoroughly cooked through and the outside leaves are golden and crisp.

Meanwhile, for the date butter, start by browning the butter. Set a nonstick pan over a medium heat. Add the butter and allow to melt; it will gently start to foam, which will take around 3 minutes. Swirl the butter gently around the pan and allow it to continue bubbling and foaming. It's important to pay very close attention, as it can go from brown to burnt very quickly. The butter will begin to smell nutty, and you'll notice brown solids at the bottom of the pan: these are caramelized milk solids, and a sign that your butter is ready. Reduce the heat to low, add the dates, oil and hawaij and allow the dates to gently soften in the butter; this should take around 2 minutes. Turn off the heat and add the lemon juice, vinegar and salt. Stir, as some of the dates will have dissolved in the butter. Keep this in a warm place until you are ready to serve.

Spread the tahini sauce over a serving dish, top with the cabbages, drizzle over the warm date butter and finally sprinkle over the coriander and Aleppo chilli.

Roast Cauliflower, Saffron Tahini & Cranberry-Chilli Oil

Pull this one out for a group; I've been known to stick a candle in it and serve it for someone's birthday. Buy the biggest cauliflower you can to maximize the effect, though two smaller ones also works. I serve it whole and carve it at the table because I love the drama.

Serves 4
—— *Vegan*

1 large cauliflower
2 tablespoons olive oil
¼ teaspoon fine sea salt, plus more to cook

For the cranberry-chilli oil
30g (1oz) dried cranberries
1 tablespoon nigella seeds
2 teaspoons Aleppo chilli flakes
¼ teaspoon ground cinnamon
1 teaspoon hot smoked paprika
½ tablespoon toasted sesame seeds
1½ tablespoons maple syrup, or agave syrup
1 tablespoon soy sauce, or tamari
½ teaspoon fine sea salt
100ml (3½fl oz) vegetable oil
100g (3½oz) shallots, halved lengthways and finely sliced
1 red chilli, halved lengthways, deseeded and finely sliced
3 garlic cloves, finely sliced

For the saffron tahini
pinch of saffron threads
2 tablespoons boiling water
½ teaspoon fine sea salt
150g (5½oz) tahini
2 tablespoons lemon juice
1 tablespoon chopped dill

Start with the cranberry-chilli oil. Soak the dried cranberries in a small bowl of hot water for 10 minutes, then drain and roughly chop.

Put the nigella seeds in a heatproof bowl with the Aleppo chilli, cinnamon, paprika, sesame seeds, maple syrup, soy and salt, setting a sieve over the top. Heat the oil in a medium-sized saucepan to 180°C (350°F) or, if you don't have a thermometer, until the oil sizzles when you drop a shallot slice in. Once ready, add your shallots and chilli, stirring every so often and cooking for 3 minutes or until they are looking soft. Add the garlic and cook for a further 3 minutes, stirring regularly to prevent catching, until the shallots are starting to turn golden and look crisp. They will continue to darken once you remove them from the oil, so it's better to under-fry than over.

Once the shallot mix is ready, pour the oil through the sieve over the spices, then transfer the shallots, garlic and chilli to a plate lined with kitchen paper to allow them to crisp up. Once completely cool, combine them with the spiced oil, then stir in the cranberries. Set aside.

Preheat the oven to 220°C fan (475°F), Gas Mark 9.

Bring a large pan of salted water to the boil. Trim most of the outer leaves off the cauliflower but leave the rest; they're delicious when they crisp up. Submerge the cauliflower, stalk side up, in the water and boil gently for 8 minutes. Transfer to a colander in the sink to drain and steam-dry, again stalk side up, for about 10 minutes.

Once the cauliflower has drained and steam-dried, transfer to a tray lined with nonstick baking paper, this time stalk side down, drizzle over the olive oil and sprinkle with the salt, rubbing them all over the cauliflower. Roast for 25–30 minutes until golden and browned.

Meanwhile, grind the saffron threads to a powder with a pestle and mortar. Add the measured boiling water, stir and allow to steep for 10 minutes. Add the salt, tahini and lemon juice and whisk to combine before slowly whisking in 60–80ml (4–4½ tablespoons) of cold water until you have a sauce the consistency of pancake batter. If it's still quite stiff, you may want to add a little more water. Stir in the dill.

To serve, transfer your cauliflower to a serving dish, pour over the saffron tahini and then serve with the cranberry-chilli oil.

Butternut Squash, Baharat Candied Chestnuts & Whipped Feta

I am not really a stuffing fan, but a stuffing-inspired sweet-savoury crunchy spiced dressing? Yes, I can get behind that. This recipe specifies goji berries, but you can sub dried barberries or cranberries, even raisins if you prefer; I just love goji for their beautiful pops of colour. Pour the candied chestnuts over the hot butternut just before serving. Vegan butter won't caramelize, so just melt it before adding the chestnuts, or use olive oil instead.

Serves 4
—— *Can be made vegan*

1 butternut squash, quartered lengthways and deseeded, then each quarter halved again
3 tablespoons olive oil
½ teaspoon fine sea salt
¼ teaspoon ground cinnamon

For the baharat candied chestnuts
30g (1oz) goji berries
80g (2¾oz) unsalted butter, or vegan alternative
180g (6oz) cooked chestnuts, chopped to a coarse crumble
1½ tablespoons baharat (for homemade, see page 19)
2 teaspoons apple cider vinegar
2 tablespoons caster sugar
½ teaspoon fine sea salt
1 tablespoon olive oil, plus more if needed

For the whipped feta
200g (7oz) feta cheese, or vegan alternative, roughly crumbled
150g (5½oz) Greek yogurt, or vegan alternative
fine sea salt (optional)

Preheat the oven to 180°C fan (400°F), Gas Mark 6. Line a baking tray with nonstick baking paper.

Toss the butternut pieces with the oil, salt and cinnamon, transfer to the lined tray and roast for around 50 minutes until cooked through and slightly coloured. They are ready when you can easily insert a knife through a piece.

Meanwhile, soak the goji berries in a small bowl of hot water for 5 minutes, then drain.

Put the butter in a nonstick saucepan and set over a medium heat. Once melted, add the chopped chestnuts, stir and gently cook until the butter starts to foam and smell nutty; this will take about 8 minutes. At this point, add the soaked goji berries, baharat, cider vinegar, sugar and salt and stir; the foam will dissipate a little and it'll look a little more homogenous. Reduce the heat to low and continue cooking until the chestnuts darken; a further 5 minutes.

Transfer to a bowl and stir in the olive oil to help cool it down and make sure it doesn't harden too much, adding the juices from the roasted butternut tray as well, if there are any. The texture of the chestnut mix should be a little loose; you can add a little more oil if it feels too stiff.

For the whipped feta, put the feta and yogurt in a blender and blitz until completely smooth, scraping down the bowl until fully incorporated. (You can also do this in a jug with a stick blender.) Season with a little salt if needs be, but it should already be salty from the cheese.

To serve, smooth the whipped feta on to serving plates, top with the butternut and pile the chestnut mixture on top of each quarter piece.

Smoked Aubergine, Harissa & Basil Lasagne

Part of the joy of this dish is the smoky aubergine, from grilling them on a gas hob or barbecue. However, it's still worth making if you're roasting the aubergines in the oven; just add 2 teaspoons sweet smoked paprika to the sauce for a smoky boost. The sauce is definitely spicy, so if you're less keen on heat, reduce the harissa to 1 tablespoon. You will need a baking dish of about 27 × 22cm (10¾ × 8½ inches).

Serves 4

4 aubergines
12 dried lasagne sheets
250g (9oz) mozzarella balls (about 2), drained and broken into rough chunks

For the harissa tomato sauce

2 tablespoons olive oil
3 garlic cloves, finely sliced
400g (14oz) can of finely chopped tomatoes
300ml (½ pint) water
1 teaspoon fine sea salt
2 tablespoons harissa
2 tablespoons mango chutney
¼ teaspoon cracked black pepper

For the basil ricotta

30g (1oz) basil, stalks and all, roughly chopped
4 tablespoons olive oil
250g (9oz) ricotta cheese
½ teaspoon fine sea salt

For the spiced crumbs

40g (1½oz) panko or dried sourdough breadcrumbs
2 tablespoons olive oil
1 teaspoon ras el hanout (for homemade, see page 18)
¼ teaspoon fine sea salt

Begin by grilling your aubergines. If you have a gas hob, set 2 rings on high and use a fork to pierce each aubergine 2–3 times so that the steam can escape. Place directly on to the flames and use tongs to rotate them every 5 minutes or so until they are completely soft and collapsed; the skins should be white when you remove them from the heat. If you don't have a gas stove, preheat the oven to 200°C fan (425°F), Gas Mark 7. Roast the aubergines on a rack in the upper one-third of the oven for 50–60 minutes until soft and squishy. (See recipe introduction for how to introduce a smoky flavour to the sauce.)

Transfer to a wire rack until cool before peeling off the skins. Once peeled, discard the stalk ends and tear the flesh into chunky strips, then press those in a clean tea towel to extract as much liquid as possible.

For the sauce, put the oil in a saucepan and set over a medium heat. Add the garlic and sauté for 1–2 minutes until it softens. Add the canned tomatoes, measured water, salt, harissa, mango chutney and pepper and cook for a further 15 minutes over a medium heat, stirring occasionally, until thickened. Taste, then set aside.

For the basil ricotta, put the basil and oil in a blender and blitz to a coarse paste, then scrape into a mixing bowl and stir in the ricotta and salt. Set aside.

Combine all the ingredients for the spiced crumbs in a bowl and stir thoroughly so that the crumbs absorb the oil.

Preheat the oven to 180°C fan (400°F), Gas Mark 6.

Spread one-third of the sauce over the oven dish (see recipe introduction), then arrange 4 lasagne sheets on top, snapping them as needed to ensure an even coverage. Dot with one-third of the ricotta mix, one-third of the torn mozzarella and then one-third of the torn aubergine. Repeat twice so that you have 3 layers of everything. Sprinkle over the spiced crumbs evenly on top.

Bake for 30 minutes until bubbling and golden.

Harissa Roast Carrots, Mango Labneh & Mint

Mango chutney is a wonder ingredient: I use it in marinades for robust, spiced fruitiness, or as here, stirred through labneh, for a highly delicious combination. This calls for half the amount of labneh from the recipe on page 24. Make half that recipe if you don't fancy leftovers, though it is great to have in the fridge for all your sandwich needs. You'll need to make the labneh the day before.

Serves 4

1kg (2lb 4oz) carrots, peeled and left whole (unless they're absolutely massive, when they can be halved lengthways)

For the marinade
2 tablespoons olive oil
1 tablespoon harissa
1 tablespoon date syrup
½ teaspoon fine sea salt

For the mint salsa
2 teaspoons nigella seeds
2 teaspoons hawaij (for homemade, see page 19)
6 tablespoons olive oil
finely grated zest of 1 unwaxed lime, plus 2 tablespoons lime juice
about 3 tablespoons finely chopped mint leaves (about 12g/½oz)
1 teaspoon fine sea salt

For the mango labneh
300g (10½oz) Labneh (see page 24 and recipe introduction)
2 tablespoons mango chutney
⅛ teaspoon ground turmeric

Preheat the oven to 200°C fan (425°F), Gas Mark 7. Line a baking tray with nonstick baking paper.

Place all the marinade ingredients in a bowl and whisk them to combine. Put the carrots on the lined tray and pour over the marinade. Use your hands to mix this all together, ensuring it's evenly dispersed. Roast for 25–30 minutes, turning once halfway through. You should be able to pass a knife through a carrot without resistance when they're done, and they should look golden. The marinade would have caught, but don't worry, this will taste great.

Meanwhile, combine all the ingredients for the mint salsa in a bowl, stir and set aside.

For the labneh, mix together the ingredients in a bowl. It's totally fine if the mango chutney is lumpy, as these chunks add bursts of sweetness.

Smooth the labneh on to a serving dish, pile your carrots on top, then spoon over the mint salsa.

Whole Roast Celeriac
with Miso Onion Gravy

A dream for the festive season, this is a high-impact dish with minimal hands-on cooking. You put it all in the oven and let it do its thing: the gravy comes together in the roasting tray and thickens as it cooks, while the celeriac infuses it with flavour. If the celeriac weighs less than 900g (2lb) and you are feeding four or more, I'd use two.

Serves 4
—— *Vegan*

1 large or 2 small celeriac (total weight 1.2kg/2lb 11oz), trimmed and peeled (see recipe introduction)
1 tablespoon olive oil
½ teaspoon fine sea salt

For the miso onion gravy
3 onions, each cut into 8 wedges
4 garlic cloves, lightly crushed
900ml (1½ pints) hot vegetable stock
2 tablespoons white miso
50g (1¾oz) preserved lemon, sliced (for homemade, see page 18)
4 tablespoons olive oil
1½ teaspoons fine sea salt
2 tablespoons agave syrup, or maple syrup
1 teaspoon hot smoked paprika
2 teaspoons ground cumin
2 teaspoons ground coriander
¼ teaspoon ground cardamom

For the preserved lemon salsa
1 tablespoon finely chopped tarragon leaves
90g (3¼oz) preserved lemon, finely chopped (for homemade, see page 18)
60g (2¼oz) blanched hazelnuts, toasted and roughly crushed
2 tablespoons olive oil
1 tablespoon maple syrup, or agave syrup
2 tablespoons lemon juice
½ teaspoon fine sea salt

Preheat the oven to 180°C fan (400°F), Gas Mark 6.

Take a deep roasting tray for which you have a wire rack that fits inside so that the celeriac can be elevated over the gravy while it roasts. Arrange the onions and garlic across the bottom. Put the remaining gravy ingredients in a bowl, whisk thoroughly to combine, then pour over the onions and garlic.

Take the celeriac and score the top of it, about 2.5cm (1-inch) deep, at 2cm (¾-inch) intervals, then score it in the other direction for a crosshatched effect. Rub with the olive oil and salt. Place the celeriac on the rack, set it over the gravy ingredients in the tray, cover tightly with foil and place in the oven for 1 hour. You should be able to slide a knife easily through the centre, so cook for a little longer if there is still some resistance.

For the salsa, put everything in a bowl and stir to combine.

Once the time is up on the celeriac, crank up the oven to its highest heat, remove the foil and roast for a further 12–15 minutes until the celeriac is golden and the gravy is thickened and bubbling. If it has reduced too much, you can add a splash of water to loosen it all.

To serve, carve the celeriac into 2.5cm (1-inch) slices, spoon over the gravy and scatter with the salsa.

—— **How to serve**

This would be lovely with some mashed potato or bread to soak up the gravy.

Hispi Cabbage, Whipped Sesame Tofu & Double Ginger

I love this way of eating cabbage cold, as it feels so fresh and the tofu and spring onions cling to it perfectly. Stem ginger may seem an odd ingredient here, but trust me. It brings something so fun and surprising, and by using its syrup in the tofu and the ginger itself in a salsa, it feels very satisfying to make. I serve this at the height of summer along with some rice.

Serves 4
— **Vegan**

3 large hispi or sweetheart cabbages
fine sea salt

For the whipped tofu
300g (10½oz) silken tofu
1 tablespoon toasted sesame oil
finely grated zest of 1 unwaxed orange, plus 1 tablespoon orange juice
1 tablespoon stem ginger syrup
1 teaspoon fine sea salt
1 tablespoon neutral-flavoured oil

For the spring onion salsa
bunch of spring onions, finely sliced
2 tablespoons toasted sesame seeds
1 tablespoon black sesame seeds
1 tablespoon Aleppo chilli flakes, or regular chilli flakes
20g (¾oz) fresh root ginger, peeled and finely grated
¼ teaspoon freshly ground white pepper
½ teaspoon fine sea salt
100ml (3½fl oz) neutral-flavoured oil
1½ tablespoons light soy sauce
2 tablespoons lime juice
80g (2¾oz) stem ginger, finely chopped

To prepare your cabbage, first remove any tougher-looking outer leaves. Use a small paring knife to remove the core from the bottom of the cabbages in a reverse cone shape, then carefully peel away the leaves, cutting more of the bottom of the cabbage as you go if you need to, in order to free them. Give them a good wash while you bring a pot of salted water to the boil. Add the leaves to the boiling water and boil for 2 minutes until they are bright green and tender. Drain in a colander and run cold water over the leaves until completely cool.

Lay a clean tea towel on a work surface and spread the cabbage over the cloth, placing another clean cloth on top and pressing to absorb as much liquid as possible. You can roll this up into a sausage and set it aside while you prepare the tofu and salsa.

To make the whipped tofu, combine all the ingredients in a blender and blend until completely smooth. Transfer to a container and chill until ready to use.

To make the salsa, place the spring onions, sesame seeds, chilli, root ginger, pepper and salt in a heatproof bowl. Put the oil in a small saucepan and set over a high heat until it is smoking. Pour this over your salsa ingredients: it should sizzle and splutter a little, so do this very slowly. Stir to combine, then stir in the soy, lime juice and chopped stem ginger.

To serve, smooth the whipped tofu over a serving dish. Arrange the cabbage leaves over this, then drizzle over the spring onion salsa.

— **How to serve**

You want to serve this cold, so it's best eaten in summer as part of a really light and fresh meal.

Whole Roast Swede & Peanut
with Grapefruit

Swede is associated with heavy wintry dishes: neeps and tatties and hearty soups. This recipe spins that notion on its head. It's vibrant and bright and will put a smile on your face in the depths of winter. If you come across a huge swede, great, use it, but they generally seem to be a little small. Aim for a total weight of 1kg (2lb 4oz) to feed four.

Serves 4
—— **Vegan**

2 swedes (total weight 1kg/2lb 4oz, or see recipe introduction)
2 tablespoons olive oil
½ teaspoon fine sea salt
sea salt flakes
50g (1¾oz) roasted salted peanuts, roughly chopped, to serve

For the peanut coriander sauce
100g (3½oz) coriander, roughly chopped, plus more leaves to serve
1 tablespoon vegan fish sauce
2 tablespoons soy sauce, or tamari
1 tablespoon sesame oil
4 tablespoons vegetable oil
2 garlic cloves, roughly chopped
4 tablespoons lime juice
3 green bird eye chillies, roughly chopped
1½ tablespoons smooth peanut butter
½ teaspoon fine sea salt
1½ tablespoons agave syrup

For the grapefruit salsa
2 grapefruits
½ red onion, finely sliced
¼ teaspoon fine sea salt
1 teaspoon sesame oil

For the maple tahini
50g (1¾oz) tahini
30g (1oz) maple syrup, or agave syrup

Preheat the oven to 180°C fan (400°F), Gas Mark 6. Line a baking tray with nonstick baking paper.

Wash the swedes thoroughly, then place on the lined tray. Season with the oil and fine salt and give them a good rub to ensure the skin is covered. Roast for 1½ hours or until you can easily insert a skewer. Allow to cool for 15 minutes or so until warm enough to handle. The skin should have blistered and come away from the flesh a little, so gently peel it off using a small knife.

Meanwhile, for the sauce, place all the ingredients in a blender and blitz until smooth but you are still able to see flecks of coriander, as you want to retain a little texture. Set aside.

For the salsa, top and tail the grapefruits and then, with one flat side on the work surface, use a sharp knife to shave off the skin, being sure to also remove the white pith. Then segment the grapefruits, cutting the segments out either side of the membranes, and roughly chop the flesh. Put it in a mixing bowl and gently stir in the remaining salsa ingredients.

Stir the tahini and maple syrup together in a bowl to combine.

To serve, carve the swede into slices. Smooth the sauce across a serving dish and top with the swede, seasoning with a pinch of sea salt flakes. Drizzle over the maple tahini, then scatter with the grapefruit salsa and chopped roasted peanuts.

—— **How to serve**

There's a lot going on here, so serving this with plain rice would be perfect.

Star Anise & Orange Braised Fennel

A head chef once told me that a good flavour pairing should reveal a little more about the main ingredient. This advice was ringing in my head when I developed this book. For me, star anise tells you so much about what it shares with fennel: aniseed spice, liquorice sweetness, herbal crispness. This feels so luxurious and indulgent. It absolutely needs to be served with rice to soak up the sauce, and a fresh salad to cut through the richness.

Serves 4
—— *Can be made vegan*

4 fennel bulbs, with tops
3 tablespoons olive oil, plus more if needed
2 tablespoons lime juice
1 tablespoon finely chopped tarragon leaves
½ teaspoon fine sea salt

For the braising stock
300ml (½ pint) vegetable stock
100ml (3½fl oz) orange juice
50g (1¾oz) caster sugar
4 star anise
2½ tablespoons tamari, or soy sauce
70g (2½oz) unsalted butter, or vegan alternative
1 teaspoon fine sea salt
30g (1oz) fresh root ginger, peeled and cut into 1cm (½-inch) coins
1 teaspoon rice vinegar

—— **How to serve**

This is lovely served with one of my rice dishes for soaking up the sauce (see pages 148 and 150), and something green and crunchy on the side is essential: I'd go for the Cucumber, Rose & Nigella Seed Salad or the Baby Gem, Tamarind Dressing & Avocado Crema (see pages 174 and 176).

Preheat the oven to 200°C fan (425°F), Gas Mark 7.

Trim the fennel tops off and set them aside for later, then cut the fennel bulbs in half vertically, removing the tough outer leaves. Put the oil in a wide frying pan and set over a medium-high heat. Once hot, add the fennel, cut sides down, and fry until golden on this side only. This will take 4-5 minutes, and you may need to do it in 2 batches, depending on the size of your pan. (Add another glug of oil for the second batch if it's looking a bit dry.) Once bronzed, place in a braising dish, again cut sides down, trying to ensure the fennel is in one layer, but don't worry if not!

Put all the ingredients for the braising stock in a saucepan and bring to the boil. Whisk the stock then pour it over the fennel and transfer, uncovered, to the oven. Roast the fennel for 30-35 minutes until you can easily pass a knife through it but it still holds its shape. Set the fennel aside, transfer the braising liquid to a saucepan and set over a high heat. Reduce for 8-9 minutes until it looks like a glossy, loose caramel. Return the fennel to the pan to gently heat through and glaze in the caramel.

Take the reserved fennel fronds and slice as finely as possible. Put these in a bowl with the lime juice, tarragon and salt and toss to combine.

To serve, transfer the fennel to a platter, pour over the caramel and scatter with the dressed fennel fronds.

Cauliflower, Bkeila Cream & Sumac Oil

Bkeila is a caramelized spinach condiment made by Tunisian Jews. The secret to its deliciousness is sautéing chopped spinach in oil for so long that it releases its natural sugars; a unique and interesting way to cook it. Here I let it down with cream, for something similar to creamed spinach... but turbocharged. Heaven on a roasted cauliflower.

Serves 6–8
— **Can be made vegan**

½ teaspoon fine sea salt, plus more to cook
2 cauliflowers
4 tablespoons vegetable oil

For the bkeila cream
260g (9¼oz) baby spinach
30g (1oz) coriander, roughly chopped
8 tablespoons olive oil
1 onion, finely chopped
4 garlic cloves, finely grated
1½ teaspoons fine sea salt
2 teaspoons cumin seeds, ground
2 teaspoons coriander seeds, ground
3 black limes, finely ground
1 teaspoon sweet smoked paprika
1 teaspoon caraway seeds, ground
1 teaspoon ground cinnamon
130ml (4fl oz) double cream, or vegan alternative
200ml (7fl oz) vegetable stock
1 teaspoon caster sugar
25g (1oz) unsalted butter, or vegan alternative
2 tablespoons lemon juice

For the sumac oil
1 tablespoon sumac
2 tablespoons olive oil
1 tablespoon lemon juice
¼ teaspoon fine sea salt

For the bkeila cream, place the spinach and coriander in a blender and blitz until coarsely chopped. (You can do this by hand; it'll just take longer.) Pour the oil into a nonstick saucepan and add the onion, garlic and salt. Sauté over a medium heat until soft; this will take about 10 minutes. Add the blended spinach and coriander, as well as the spices. Cook gently, stirring regularly, for 20–30 minutes until the spinach is dark brown in colour and starting to catch. Add the cream, stock and sugar and simmer for a further 10 minutes until thickened. Stir in the butter and lemon juice, then set aside.

Bring a large saucepan of water to the boil and season with 1 teaspoon salt. If you have a pan big enough to fit 2 cauliflowers, great, but if not, you may need to do this stage twice (sorry). Trim most of the outer leaves off the cauliflowers but leave the rest; they're delicious when they crisp up. Submerge the cauliflowers, stalk side up, in the water and boil for 10 minutes. Transfer to a colander in the sink to drain and steam-dry, again stalk side up, for about 10 minutes.

Meanwhile, preheat the oven to 220°C fan (475°F), Gas Mark 9. Line a baking tray with nonstick baking paper.

Tip the cauliflowers on to the lined tray, drizzle over the oil and sprinkle with the salt, making sure it's evenly distributed. Roast in the oven for 20 minutes until golden.

Meanwhile, stir together all the ingredients for the sumac oil in a small bowl.

Transfer the cauliflower to a serving dish, pour over the bkeila sauce and drizzle with the sumac oil.

Baharat Ratatouille
with Preserved Lemon

In no way a traditional ratatouille (obviously), this is more of a ragu. The idea came to me when friends asked me to come up with a one-bowl meal for an event we catered. The idea of the event was that you could ask for seconds if you wanted... we did not anticipate all 250 guests taking us up on the offer.

Serves 4
—— *Vegan*

4 aubergines
160g (5¾oz) grilled peppers from a jar, roughly chopped
500g (1lb 2oz) courgettes, halved vertically, then halved horizontally
½ teaspoon fine sea salt
2 tablespoons olive oil

For the tomato sauce
3 tablespoons olive oil
1 onion, finely chopped
3 garlic cloves, finely sliced
1½ teaspoons fine sea salt
30g (1oz) basil, leaves and stalks kept separate, stalks finely chopped
1 tablespoon tomato purée
1½ tablespoons baharat (for homemade, see page 19)
1 teaspoon dried rosemary, finely chopped
3 tablespoons pomegranate molasses
400g (14oz) can of chopped tomatoes

For the preserved lemon salsa
3 tablespoons olive oil
60g (2¼oz) preserved lemon, finely chopped (for homemade, see page 18)
½ teaspoon fine sea salt
1 tablespoon red wine vinegar
½ tablespoon agave syrup

—— **How to serve**

At the event for which I invented this, we served it with Tahini Sauce (see page 46) and bread, which I highly recommend, but if you're looking for something a little more filling, its great with rice.

If you have a gas hob, begin by grilling your aubergines as on page 33. If you don't have a gas hob, preheat your oven to 200°C fan (425°F), Gas Mark 7. Line a baking tray with nonstick baking paper. Prick the aubergines a few times with a fork then place them whole on the lined tray. Roast for 50-60 minutes, turning occasionally, until the skin is charred and collapsed and the flesh feels completely soft. Once they're cool enough to handle, peel off the skin and discard it. Scoop out the tender flesh and discard any overly seedy or stringy parts, then transfer to a sieve set over a bowl and allow any excess liquid to drain, pressing down with a ladle to help extract as much as possible.

To make the sauce, heat the olive oil in a pan and add the onion, garlic and salt. Sauté gently for 12 minutes or until totally soft but without any colour. Add the basil stalks, tomato purée, baharat, rosemary and pomegranate molasses and cook for another 3 minutes until it has darkened a little and is beginning to sizzle and catch. Add the canned tomatoes and one-quarter of a can of water, as well as the aubergine flesh and peppers. Simmer gently for 15 minutes, stirring occasionally, until the water has evaporated and you have a rich ragu.

Meanwhile, for the salsa, finely slice the reserved basil leaves, put them in a bowl with all the other ingredients and stir to combine.

To cook the courgettes, lay them cut sides up and sprinkle with the salt. Leave for 5 minutes, then pat dry and heat the oil in a large nonstick frying pan over a high heat. Place the courgettes in the pan cut sides down and fry for 8-10 minutes until deeply browned. Flip over and cook for a further 2 minutes. This will give you quite an al dente courgette, but by all means cook them further if you wish them to be softer.

To serve, place your ragu in serving dishes, top with the courgettes and drizzle over the preserved lemon salsa.

Butternut Squash & Pilpelchuma
with Charred Corn

Pilpelchuma is a fiery paste that originated in the Libyan Jewish community and is a close cousin to other spicy North African condiments such as harissa and chermoula. This version is relatively mild, so swap the Aleppo for regular chilli flakes if you want more heat. I keep it in my fridge and use it as chilli sauce, so double up the recipe if you fancy doing the same; it will store for one week.

Serves 4
— **Vegan**

2 garlic bulbs
5 tablespoons olive oil
1 large butternut squash
½ teaspoon fine sea salt

For the pilpelchuma
30g (1oz) dried guajillo chillies (about 10)
1½ teaspoons cumin seeds
1 teaspoon caraway seeds
2 teaspoons Aleppo chilli flakes (or see recipe introduction)
½ teaspoon hot smoked paprika
½ tablespoon toasted sesame seeds
7 tablespoons olive oil
2 teaspoons chipotle paste
1 tablespoon maple syrup, or agave syrup
1½ teaspoons fine sea salt
4 tablespoons lemon juice

For the charred corn
2 sweetcorn cobs, husks removed, kernels shaved off with a sharp knife
2 tablespoons lime juice
1 tablespoon olive oil
¼ teaspoon fine sea salt
1 garlic clove, finely grated
15g (½oz) coriander, finely chopped
1 spring onion, finely sliced on the diagonal

Preheat the oven to 180°C fan (400°F), Gas Mark 6.

Cut the tops off the garlic bulbs and place them on a sheet of foil. Drizzle the exposed garlic with 1 tablespoon of the olive oil each, then tightly wrap with the foil. Roast for 30 minutes until soft and squishy, then set aside to cool completely.

Halve the squash horizontally, then vertically, remove the seeds and cut each quarter into 2 so that you have 8 pieces in total. Place on a baking tray lined with nonstick baking paper, drizzle with the remaining 3 tablespoons of olive oil and season with the salt. Roast for 50 minutes until nicely coloured and cooked all the way through.

Meanwhile, prepare your pilpelchuma. Set a frying pan over a high heat and, once hot, add the guajillo chillies and toast for about 1 minute until fragrant, tossing halfway through. Transfer to a bowl, cover with boiling water and leave to soak for 10 minutes. In a spice grinder or a high-powered bullet blender, grind all the dried spices and sesame seeds to a powder. Pop the soft garlic out of its skins and transfer this to a blender with the ground spices (unless the spices are already in a blender), along with the remaining pilpelchuma ingredients, then blitz until you have a very smooth paste.

Place a saucepan over a high heat and toast the corn kernels for 3-4 minutes until charred and toasty, tossing frequently. Transfer to a bowl and toss with the lime juice, olive oil, salt, garlic, coriander and spring onions.

Place the roast butternut on a serving dish, spoon over the pilpelchuma and sprinkle with the corn.

The Main Event

Beetroot, Olive & Date Tatin

Definitely for fans of sweet-savoury mixes. If you'd rather not get too messy peeling and roasting beetroots, you can use the cooked variety from the supermarket and just skip the pre-roasting part of the recipe.

Serves 4
—— **Can be made vegan**

500g raw beetroot, stalks trimmed, peeled and sliced into 5mm (¼-inch) rounds (or see recipe introduction)
2 tablespoons olive oil
½ teaspoon fine sea salt
good grind of black pepper
40g (1½oz) pitted kalamata olives, roughly chopped
80g (3oz) medjool dates, pitted and roughly chopped
320g (11¼oz) sheet of puff pastry
sea salt flakes, to serve

For the date caramel
50g (1¾oz) unsalted butter, or vegan alternative
2 tablespoons date syrup
3 tablespoons balsamic vinegar
2 tablespoons light soy sauce
2 garlic cloves, finely grated
¼ teaspoon fine sea salt

Preheat the oven to 180°C fan (400°F), Gas Mark 6. Line a baking sheet with nonstick baking paper.

Toss the beetroot with the oil, salt and pepper in a bowl, then transfer to the lined tray and roast for 12–15 minutes until the beetroot has softened but has not coloured. Remove from the oven and set aside.

Increase the oven temperature to 200°C fan (425°F), Gas Mark 7.

Now for the caramel. Set a 28cm (11-inch) ovenproof cast-iron pan over a medium heat and add your butter, heating until it melts. Whisk in the date syrup, balsamic, soy, garlic and salt to combine. Allow to bubble for a couple of minutes, then turn off the heat.

Arrange the beetroot slices in a circular pattern over the caramel, starting from the outer edge of the pan and working your way inwards, slightly overlapping each slice as you go to create a full, even layer. Sprinkle over the olives and dates, then cover this with the puff pastry sheet, laying it gently over the beetroot and folding the edges into the corners rusticly. Press the edges of the pastry down around the sides to seal, then use a sharp knife to cut a few small steam holes in the centre. Bake for 12–15 minutes until the pastry is golden and crisp.

Once the tart is ready, let it sit for 10 minutes and then use a palette knife to release the pastry from the sides of the pan, running it the whole way around. The pan will still be hot, so use a cloth to hold the handles, then carefully upturn it on to a plate or chopping board, tapping the pan gently to release the tart. Lightly sprinkle over a pinch of sea salt flakes, then cut the tart into 4 and transfer to plates.

—— **How to serve**

The only accompaniment I'd add is a crisp green salad and a little pot of crème fraîche on the side.

Saffron-braised Fennel, Cumin Yogurt & Olives

I know saffron is expensive, but it really shines here, infusing a caramel sauce that the fennel absorbs so well. It is worth picking up the thickest Greek yogurt you can find for this recipe; I like the 5% fat variety. If you have some labneh (see page 24 for homemade), you can use 350g (12oz) of that instead of straining the Greek yogurt as in the recipe below.

Serves 4

120g (4¼oz) unsalted butter
80g (2¾oz) caster sugar
½ teaspoon fine sea salt
1½ tablespoons white miso
1 tablespoon sherry vinegar
pinch of saffron threads
500ml (18fl oz) water
4 fennel bulbs, tops removed
sea salt flakes, to serve

For the cumin yogurt
500g (1lb 2oz) Greek yogurt
¼ teaspoon fine sea salt
80g (2¾oz) preserved lemon, finely chopped
 (for homemade, see page 18)
1 teaspoon ground cumin

For the kalamata olive salsa
170g (6oz) kalamata olives, pitted and finely chopped
1 garlic clove, finely grated
1½ tablespoons sherry vinegar
1½ tablespoons soy sauce, or tamari
2 teaspoons orange blossom water (optional)
30g (1oz) parsley leaves, finely chopped
7 tablespoons olive oil

Preheat the oven to 180°C fan (400°F), Gas Mark 6.

Start with the cumin yogurt. Stir together the yogurt and salt, then line a sieve set over a small bowl with a muslin and spoon in the yogurt. Fold over the cloth to cover, then place a few heavy bowls over the yogurt to help it strain quickly. Leave this for at least 2 hours.

For the saffron braising liquid, add the butter to a 30cm (12-inch) ovenproof cast-iron pan for which you have a lid. Add the sugar, salt, miso, vinegar and saffron along with the measured water. Bring to the boil, whisking the mixture until the sugar and salt have dissolved before turning off the heat.

Halve your fennel, removing any tough outer layers, then halve again so that each bulb is split into 4. Transfer the fennel to the saffron mix, ensuring it's half-submerged in the liquid and topping up with a little water if needs be. Cover with the lid, then place in the oven and cook for 30 minutes until the fennel is soft and cooked through: you can test this by seeing if a knife goes through it easily. Remove the fennel with a slotted spoon and set aside.

Place the pan with the saffron mixture over a high heat and reduce it rapidly for 12 minutes until it forms a thick caramel that coats the back of a spoon. Turn off the heat and return the fennel, tossing to coat.

To make the salsa, put all the ingredients in a small bowl and stir together.

Put the strained yogurt in a mixing bowl and stir in the preserved lemon and cumin.

Smooth the strained yogurt on to a serving platter, then place the glazed fennel pieces on top, pouring over the remaining reduced saffron caramel. Spoon over the kalamata salsa and finish with a pinch of sea salt flakes.

Leeks & Kiwi Salsa Verde
with Chipotle Pecans

Mexican salsa verde is usually made with tomatillos, which are also known as husk tomatoes. These are green, very tangy and sour. They are tough to find in the UK, so I like to use kiwis in their place, which adds a similar sharpness and zing.

Serves 4
—— **Vegan**

1kg (2lb 4oz) leeks, trimmed
3 tablespoons olive oil
½ teaspoon fine sea salt
good grind of black pepper
200ml (7fl oz) vegetable stock

For the kiwi salsa verde
½ onion, quartered
3 garlic cloves, peeled
1 red bird eye chilli, halved lengthways and deseeded
2 tablespoons water
30g (1oz) coriander, roughly chopped
3 tablespoons olive oil
½ avocado, destoned, peeled and roughly chopped
1 kiwi, peeled and roughly chopped
2 tablespoons lime juice
1 teaspoon fine sea salt

For the chipotle pecans
1 tablespoon olive oil
1 teaspoon chipotle paste
½ tablespoon maple syrup, or agave syrup
¼ teaspoon fine sea salt
70g (2½oz) pecans, roughly chopped

For the pickled kiwi
1 kiwi, peeled, quartered and finely sliced
1 tablespoon lime juice

—— **How to serve**

This would be really fun served alongside some refried beans, rice and tortilla chips.

Cut the leeks in half horizontally, before cutting these lengths in half vertically. Soak these in cold water for 10 minutes to get rid of any grit.

Meanwhile, make the salsa verde. Set a frying pan over a high heat. Once the pan is smoking hot, add the onion, garlic and chilli. Sear until blistered for about 3 minutes before turning everything over with tongs and blistering for a further 3 minutes. Remove the garlic and chilli to a bowl, as they colour the quickest, then give the onion a further 2 minutes on the last remaining side they need to be grilled. Remove the onion to the bowl with the garlic and chilli and set aside until completely cool.

Tip the charred ingredients into a blender, ideally a high-powered bullet type. Add the measured water and pulse-blend to a smooth paste. Add the remaining salsa verde ingredients and blend again until smooth, then set aside.

Preheat the oven to 180°C fan (400°F), Gas Mark 6.

Drain the cleaned leeks, lay them out, cut-side up, on a deep-sided baking tray and season with the oil, salt and pepper. Pour in the stock before covering tightly with foil and roasting for 25 minutes until the leeks are soft and cooked through.

Meanwhile, prepare the chipotle pecans. Mix together the oil, chipotle paste, maple syrup and salt in a small bowl. Add the pecans and coat them in the marinade before transferring to a baking tray lined with nonstick baking paper. Roast for 7 minutes until toasty and slightly caramelized. Set aside to cool.

Next make the pickled kiwi. Marinate the kiwi slices in the lime juice for 5 minutes.

Uncover the leeks, increase the oven temperature to 220°C fan (475°F), Gas Mark 9 and return to the oven for a further 8 minutes until nicely charred and a little crisp.

To serve the dish, smooth the salsa verde on to serving dishes and arrange the leeks on top. Finally, scatter over the pickled kiwi and toasted chipotle pecans.

Sweet Potatoes, Amba & Orange Blossom

This is layer upon layer of big flavours, and can really stand alone, or be served just with some lemony green beans. It's great on a wintry day, as the bright, vibrant flavours are transportative when climes are feeling a little dull and grey.

Serves 4

—— *Can be made vegan*

4 sweet potatoes

For the amba & orange blossom butter

115g (4oz) unsalted butter, or vegan alternative
80g (2¾oz) medjool dates, pitted and roughly chopped
80g (2¾oz) preserved lemon, finely chopped (for homemade, see page 18)
3 tablespoons amba
1 tablespoon white wine vinegar
1 teaspoon orange blossom water
½ teaspoon fine sea salt

To serve

4 tablespoons Greek yogurt, or soured cream, or vegan alternative
2 tablespoons harissa
60g (2¼oz) toasted pecans, roughly chopped

Preheat the oven to 180°C fan (400°F), Gas Mark 6. Line a baking tray with nonstick baking paper.

Gently prick the sweet potatoes with a fork and place them on the lined tray. Roast for about 1 hour or until you can pass a knife through them easily.

To make the amba butter, put the butter, dates and preserved lemon in a saucepan and set over a medium heat for 4–5 minutes until the dates have broken down and turned into a bit of a paste, stirring regularly. Turn off the heat and stir in the amba, vinegar, orange blossom water and salt. It should come together into a thick, yellow sauce.

Transfer your potatoes to a serving dish, split them open and fill each with one-quarter of the amba butter. Top each with 1 tablespoon of yogurt, a ½ tablespoon drizzle of harissa and some chopped toasted pecans.

—— *How to serve*

Eat with a sharply dressed green salad to cut through the richness.

On the Side

Black Garlic & Lemon Pilaf

This pilaf is so flavourful that it can stand on its own, if you want a deeply satisfying rice dish that offers heavy-hitting umami. This is a riff on one of the first dishes I worked on at the Ottolenghi Test Kitchen. I cannot tell you how nervous I was making this, and the utter relief when it got the thumbs-up from Yotam.

Serves 4

—— *Vegan*

4 tablespoons olive oil
3 onions, each cut into 6 wedges
2 teaspoons fine sea salt
1 tablespoon cumin seeds
zest of 1 unwaxed lemon, shaved off in strips with a vegetable peeler
1 cinnamon stick
300g (10½oz) basmati rice, washed until the water runs clear
50g (1¾oz) black garlic, finely sliced
525ml (19fl oz) boiling water
60g (2¼oz) raisins (optional)
250g (9oz) cooked Puy lentils (from a pouch is fine here)

Set a saucepan for which you have a lid over a medium heat and add the oil. Once it's hot, add the onion wedges and salt and sauté gently until the onions have softened and slightly coloured; this will take around 25 minutes. Add the cumin seeds, lemon zest strips and cinnamon stick and sauté for 5 minutes more until fragrant.

Add the drained rice and black garlic and toast them for 2 minutes, stirring regularly, before adding the measured boiling water. Stir, bring back to the boil, then clamp on the lid and reduce the heat to low. Allow to cook gently for 15 minutes.

Meanwhile, soak the raisins, if using, in a small bowl of hot water for 10 minutes, then drain.

Once the rice has had its 15 minutes, turn off the heat. Lift the lid, stir in the drained raisins, if using, and the lentils, then cover with a clean tea towel. Clamp the lid back on over the cloth and allow to steam for 10 minutes before serving.

—— ***How to serve***

Accompany this dish simply with fried eggs and a little garlicky yogurt.

Magic Rice

'Magic' because of the lack of ingredients (I'm pretty proud of myself for my uncharacteristic restraint here) and the high level of impact. My love for caramelized onions could probably span well into a second book (and if that goes for you too, I hope you've already made my Ashkenazi Egg Mayonnaise, see page 56).

Serves 4
—— *Vegan*

80ml (2¾fl oz) neutral-flavoured oil
3 onions, finely chopped
½ teaspoon ground turmeric
2 teaspoons fine sea salt
300g (10½oz) basmati rice, washed until the water runs clear
525ml (19fl oz) boiling water

Put the oil in a saucepan for which you have a lid and set it over a medium-low heat. Add the onions and sauté for around 30 minutes, stirring frequently, until deep golden in colour.

Add the turmeric and salt and sauté for a minute or so.

Now tip in the drained rice and toast it for 2 minutes, stirring regularly, then pour in the measured boiling water. Stir, bring to the boil, then clamp on the lid and reduce the heat to low. Allow the rice to cook gently for 15 minutes.

Once this time has elapsed, turn off the heat, lift the lid and cover the pot with a clean tea towel, then clamp the lid back on over the cloth and allow to steam for 10 minutes before serving.

—— **How to serve**

This goes with everything, but I especially love to eat it with the Star Anise & Orange Braised Fennel (see page 130). And, to let you into a bit of a secret, this, slathered with tahini, never fails to bring me back to my senses whether I'm suffering from a hangover or whatever else. Magic indeed.

Toasted Buckwheat Tabbouleh

Not a traditional tabbouleh by any stretch of the imagination, instead this offers a little wink to its namesake. I've only come to toasted buckwheat recently, but the smoky, nutty flavour imparts so much that it's become a bit of a staple. You can find it in health food shops or Eastern European grocers, where it may be labelled *kasha*.

Serves 4–6
—— *Vegan*

1 teaspoon fine sea salt, plus more to cook the buckwheat
200g (7oz) toasted buckwheat (see recipe introduction)
30g (1oz) barberries, or goji berries
60g (2¼oz) parsley, finely chopped
30g (1oz) coriander, finely chopped
20g (¾oz) mint leaves, finely chopped
70ml (2⅓fl oz) olive oil
4 tablespoons lemon juice
2 tablespoons soy sauce, or tamari
1 tablespoon toasted sesame oil
1 tablespoon agave syrup, or maple syrup

Bring a saucepan of salted water to the boil and add your toasted buckwheat, then cook according to the packet instructions until tender (usually about 12 minutes). Drain into a sieve, then rinse under cold water until completely cooled. Shake the sieve to ensure the buckwheat is as dry as possible before transferring to a large bowl.

Meanwhile, soak the barberries in a small bowl of hot water for 10 minutes, then drain.

Stir the barberries and all the remaining ingredients into the buckwheat, not forgetting the 1 teaspoon of salt, before transferring to a serving dish.

Potato Salad & Basil Zhoug
with Coconut Crunch

There are a few components here; I would recommend making them all ahead of time and assembling the salad on the day. The coconut crunch recipe produces more than you will need for this, but it's so good it'll be something you'll want to keep in your larder for making simple salads or roasted vegetables taste immeasurably better. It will keep for a month in a cool, dark place.

Serves 6
—— *Can be made vegan*

1.25kg (2lb 12oz) Desiree or Yukon Gold potatoes, peeled and cut into 1.5cm (5/8-inch) cubes
1 teaspoon fine sea salt
1 quantity Basil Zhoug (see page 47)
½ red onion, finely chopped

For the garlic & lemon dressing
2½ tablespoons lemon juice
50g (1¾oz) mayonnaise, or vegan alternative
100g (3½oz) Greek yogurt, or vegan alternative
3 garlic cloves, finely grated
1 teaspoon fine sea salt

For the coconut crunch
80g (2¾oz) pumpkin seeds, toasted and roughly chopped
30g (1oz) desiccated coconut
2 tablespoons toasted sesame oil
2 tablespoons maple syrup, or agave syrup
2 teaspoons chilli flakes
1 teaspoon fine sea salt

Put the potatoes in a pan with the 1 teaspoon of fine sea salt, then pour in enough cold water to cover by 2.5cm (1 inch). Bring to the boil, then cook for 12–15 minutes until totally tender all the way through. Drain and allow to steam-dry for 10 minutes in a colander set over a bowl.

To make the dressing, whisk together all the ingredients in a large bowl.

Once the potatoes have steam-dried but are still warm, add them to the dressing, toss thoroughly and set aside.

To make the coconut crunch, set a small saucepan over a medium heat and add all the ingredients. Stir continuously for 2½–3 minutes until the coconut has browned and it's looking a little more glossy and sticky. Transfer to a bowl to cool.

To the dressed potatoes add the basil zhoug and red onion. Toss gently but thoroughly before transferring everything to a serving plate and scattering with half the coconut crunch.

Lime Pickle & Miso Roasted Sweet Potato

The perfect sweet potato side dish, brought alive by a few store-cupboard staples. It looks very unassuming, like plain roast potato. But that's a big part of what makes this dish so joyful: the complete surprise about the level of flavour it's secretly packing.

Serves 4
—— *Can be made vegan*

3 sweet potatoes, peeled and cut into 2.5cm (1-inch) chunks
2 tablespoons olive oil
½ teaspoon fine sea salt

For the miso glaze
2 tablespoons lime pickle
2 tablespoons agave syrup, or honey, or maple syrup
1 tablespoon miso (white or red both work)
1 garlic clove, finely grated
1½ tablespoons water

For the lime pickle yogurt
1 tablespoon lime pickle
150g (5½oz) Greek yogurt, or vegan alternative

For the sesame-dressed coriander
2 teaspoons toasted sesame oil
juice of 1 lime
15g (½oz) coriander, roughly chopped
⅛ teaspoon fine sea salt

Preheat the oven to 180°C fan (400°F), Gas Mark 6. Line a baking tray with nonstick baking paper.

Place the sweet potatoes on the lined tray and toss with the olive oil and salt, then spread out in a single layer and roast for 25 minutes until cooked through and beginning to colour. Remove from the oven.

Increase the oven temperature to 200°C fan (425°F), Gas Mark 7.

Blitz all the ingredients for the glaze in a blender, ideally a high-powered bullet blender, until completely smooth. Add to the sweet potatoes and toss to coat, then return to the oven for a further 10 minutes until bubbly and caramelized. Transfer to a serving dish.

Gently ripple the lime pickle into the yogurt and spoon into a separate serving bowl.

Stir the ingredients for the sesame-dressed coriander together in a bowl, then scatter this over the roasted sweet potatoes and serve, with the yogurt on the side.

—— **How to serve**

I like to eat this alongside the Toasted Buckwheat Tabbouleh and a dish of roast carrots (see pages 153, 109 and 122).

Hawaij Roast Potatoes
with Preserved Lemon Roast Shallots

This recipe is the main reason why I always have hawaij in my cupboard. Its ability to elevate roast potatoes and imbue them with an even more golden hue is quite striking. You can make the roast shallots ahead of time and just scatter them on to the potatoes when they're ready; the residual heat will warm them up.

Serves 4-6
—— **Vegan**

2kg (4lb 8oz) Maris Piper potatoes, peeled and each cut into 4cm (1½-inch) chunks
½ tablespoon fine sea salt, plus more to cook the potatoes
150ml (¼ pint) olive oil
1 tablespoon hawaij (for homemade, see page 19)

For the roast shallots
600g (1lb 5oz) banana shallots, halved lengthways
2 tablespoons olive oil
½ teaspoon fine sea salt
1 garlic clove, finely grated
30g (1oz) parsley leaves, finely chopped
2 tablespoons lemon juice
120g (4¼oz) preserved lemon, finely chopped (for homemade, see page 18)

Preheat the oven to 180°C fan (400°F), Gas Mark 6.

Cover the potatoes in salted water in a large saucepan and set over a high heat. Once boiling, set a timer for 11–12 minutes. By this point, the potatoes should be cooked through, and a knife should slide easily through them. Transfer to a colander in the sink and let them steam-dry for 10 minutes.

Meanwhile, place the shallots, oil and salt in a roasting tin and toss to combine. Roast for 12 minutes until golden and soft. Leave to cool for 15 minutes or so before tossing with the remaining roast shallot ingredients.

Back to the potatoes. Put the olive oil in a large roasting tin and heat in the oven for 10 minutes. Give the potatoes a shake in the colander for a minute, roughing up the edges, to ensure more surface area for crispiness. Don't worry if they fall apart a bit. Remove the heated oil from the oven – it should be smoking at this point – and use a large spoon to carefully lower the potatoes into the oil, which will sizzle upon contact. Sprinkle over the ½ tablespoon of salt and the hawaij, then toss the potatoes in the oil so that they are evenly covered with seasoning. Roast for 40 minutes, tossing once halfway through, until golden and crisp.

Use a slotted spoon to transfer the potatoes to a serving dish, then scatter with the roast shallot mixture to serve.

Amba Butter Beans, Sage & Garlic Crisp

A subtle exercise in amba's magical ability to add fruity acidity to rich dishes; a little goes a long way here. The quality of beans is crucial; canned beans just don't cut it when you're serving them so simply. Bold Bean Co is my brand of choice, but any jarred varieties work nicely here. If you can't track down amba, replace it with 1 tablespoon of lemon juice.

Serves 3
—— **Can be made vegan**

100ml (3½fl oz) crème fraîche, or vegan alternative
1 tablespoon lemon juice
1 teaspoon amba (or see recipe introduction)
¼ teaspoon fine sea salt
1 garlic clove, finely grated
570g (1lb 4½oz) jar of butter beans, drained and rinsed (400g/14oz drained weight)

For the sage & garlic crisp
8 tablespoons olive oil
20 sage leaves, finely sliced
4 garlic cloves, finely sliced
1 red chilli, halved lengthways, deseeded and finely sliced
¼ teaspoon fine sea salt

For the sage and garlic crisp, heat the oil in a small saucepan set over a medium heat. Add the sage, sliced garlic and chilli and fry for 7–8 minutes, stirring regularly, until the sage is crisp and the garlic is starting to look golden. Remember the garlic will continue to colour after you take it off the heat, so it's best to err on the side of caution here. Transfer everything to a bowl, stir in the salt and set aside.

In a separate medium-sized bowl, mix together the crème fraîche, lemon juice, amba, salt and grated garlic, then gently stir in the beans. Transfer to a serving dish, spreading the beans out in a single layer, then drizzle over the sage and garlic crisp.

Ful Medames, Harissa Roast Tomatoes & Pickled Chilli Salsa

My non-traditional take on this Egyptian dish, usually served at breakfast, but breakfast, lunch or dinner, ful medames has got your back. Fava beans can be bought in Middle Eastern supermarkets. You can also find dried fava (which you would need to pre-cook) in health food shops; just soak 400g (14oz), as they double in weight after cooking, and reserve 600ml (20fl oz) of the cooking liquid to add to the pot in addition to the 300ml (½ pint) water added later in the recipe.

Serves 6
—— *Vegan*

2 × 400g (14oz) cans of fava beans (or see recipe introduction)
5 garlic cloves, finely chopped
1½ tablespoons ground cumin
5 tablespoons tahini paste
1 teaspoon fine sea salt
1 teaspoon sweet smoked paprika
300ml (½ pint) water
4 tablespoons lemon juice
olive oil, to serve (optional)

For the harissa roast tomatoes
500g (1lb 2oz) cherry or baby plum tomatoes
2 tablespoons olive oil
½ teaspoon fine sea salt
2 tablespoons harissa

For the pickled chilli salsa
½ red onion, finely chopped
4 tablespoons olive oil
finely grated zest of 1 unwaxed lemon, plus 2 tablespoons lemon juice
1 tablespoon chopped basil leaves
40g (1½oz) whole pickled chillies, finely chopped
½ teaspoon fine sea salt

Preheat the oven to 180°C fan (400°F), Gas Mark 6. Line a baking tray with nonstick baking paper.

For the roast tomatoes, toss the tomatoes together with the oil, salt and harissa in a bowl, then transfer to the lined tray. Roast for 25–30 minutes, tossing halfway through, until jammy and soft.

Put the fava beans and their liquid in a saucepan, along with the garlic, cumin, tahini, salt, paprika and measured water. Set over a medium heat, bring to a simmer and cook for 15 minutes, stirring occasionally. Use a potato masher to lightly crush some of the beans while they cook; this will help to thicken the sauce. The texture should have become much thicker, but should also remain loose enough to spoon. Turn off the heat and stir in the lemon juice.

To make the salsa, combine all the ingredients in a small bowl and stir to combine.

To serve, spoon the warm ful medames into a serving dish and scatter the tomatoes and salsa on top, drizzling over olive oil, if you like.

—— *How to serve*

This makes a great side dish, especially good with Harissa Roast Carrots, Mango Labneh & Mint (see page 122). But it is also an amazing stand-alone dish (when it will serve four), or, when served alongside hummus or feta, to be eaten with some lovely flatbreads and lashings of olive oil.

Confit Latkes & Soured Cream
with Baharat Apple Butter

A traditional Ashkenazi Jewish dish, typically eaten at Chanukah but bloody delicious all year round. I have given the regular apple sauce a twist to add layers of complexity, but go ahead and serve these with shop-bought apple sauce if pushed for time. Some may be surprised about the lack of egg in the latkes, but I've found that the potato starch is enough to bind them and makes for a lighter result.

Makes 15
—— **Can be made vegan**

1.5kg (3lb 5oz) Maris Piper potatoes, peeled
2 onions, halved
1½ teaspoons freshly ground white pepper
1½ tablespoons fine sea salt
vegetable oil, to fry the latkes

For the baharat apple butter
800g (1lb 12oz) Granny Smith apples, peeled, cored and cut into 1cm (½-inch) cubes
4 tablespoons apple cider vinegar
2 teaspoons baharat (for homemade, see page 19)
3 tablespoons date syrup
1 teaspoon fine sea salt
4 tablespoons water

To serve
300g (10½oz) soured cream, or vegan alternative
bunch of chives, finely chopped

To make the apple butter, place all the ingredients in a saucepan for which you have a lid and set over a medium heat. Cook down for about 15 minutes with the lid on, stirring every 5 minutes, until the apples have broken down into a mush. Remove the lid and cook for a further 10 minutes, again stirring regularly, until all the liquid has evaporated and the apples have turned into a smooth, glossy sauce. You will still have a few lumps, but that's okay. Decant into a bowl and set aside to cool.

Grate the potatoes and onions and transfer to a sieve lined with a clean tea towel set above a mixing bowl. Gather the ends of the towel together and squeeze the mix over the sieve until you have removed as much moisture as possible. Transfer the squeezed potatoes to a fresh mixing bowl, add the white pepper and salt and mix thoroughly to combine. In the bowl containing the potato liquid, the starch from the potatoes will settle on the bottom of the bowl, forming a sludge. Tip off the water, add the residual starch in the bottom of the bowl to the potatoes and mix thoroughly. It may not feel like the mixture is 'wet' enough to hold when frying, compared to when using eggs, but have faith.

Heat a 2.5cm (1-inch) depth of vegetable oil in a wide frying pan over a medium–low heat. Preheat the oven to 100°C fan (250°F), Gas Mark ½ and put a baking tray inside.

Once the oil is hot, form the latkes into roughly 80g (2¾oz) patties (once flattened, they should be the size of your palms). Squeeze between your palms to release any remaining liquid you can, then lower them into the oil; you should be able to fit about 5 latkes per batch.

Fry the latkes low and slow for about 10 minutes until they are a deep golden colour before flipping and frying for a further 10 or so minutes on the other side to the same colour. Don't be tempted to rush this step and fry at a higher temperature, as you may risk them being crisp on the outside but uncooked in the middle.

Transfer the cooked latkes to the baking tray in the warm oven to keep warm while you fry the rest, topping up the oil as necessary as you go.

Put the soured cream in a serving bowl.

Serve the latkes with the soured cream and apple butter for dipping, scattering over the chopped chives.

Okra & Curried Onions
with Barberry Dressing

We've all had miserable, slimy okra. The secret to the perfect, crisp texture is to fry it at a high heat very quickly, making this is a quick and easy side. Fry your okra in a wide pan so that it's in a single layer, allowing it to crisp up. Chopped cranberries are fine here if you can't find any barberries.

Serves 4
—— *Vegan*

4 tablespoons neutral-flavoured oil
2 onions, halved and finely sliced
2 teaspoons fine sea salt
2 garlic cloves, finely sliced
1 tablespoon plus 1 teaspoon hot curry powder
525g (1lb 3oz) okra, stalks removed, cut into 1.5cm (⅝-inch) pieces

For the barberry dressing
20g (¾oz) barberries (or see recipe introduction)
1 tablespoon olive oil
1 tablespoon soy sauce, or tamari
2 tablespoons agave syrup
½ teaspoon fine sea salt
1 teaspoon Aleppo chilli flakes, or regular chilli flakes
2 tablespoons lime juice
4 tablespoons vegetable oil
2 white onions, peeled, halved and finely sliced
2 garlic cloves, finely sliced
2 teaspoons fine sea salt

For the dressing, soak the barberries in a small bowl of hot water for 5 minutes, then drain them.

Tip the drained barberries into a small bowl, add all the other dressing ingredients and whisk together to combine. Set aside.

Heat 3 tablespoons of the oil in a frying pan set over a medium heat. Add the onions and 1 teaspoon of the salt and sauté gently for 9–10 minutes, stirring occasionally and adding the garlic halfway through, until softened and slightly coloured. Add the curry powder and cook this out for a further minute.

Use a slotted spoon to remove the onions and set aside in a bowl. Increase the temperature under the frying pan to high, adding the remaining 1 tablespoon of oil. Once the oil is smoking, add the okra and the remaining 1 teaspoon of salt and fry for 7–8 minutes, tossing frequently so that it colours evenly. You are looking for it to take on colour and appear a little burnished and crisp.

Once ready, return the onions to the pan and toss for another minute or so, allowing them to heat through and all the flavours to mix. Transfer to a platter and spoon over the barberry dressing.

—— *How to serve*

This dish packs quite a punch flavour-wise, so it would be great just with some plain rice and a fried egg, to let it really shine.

Kohlrabi & Sesame Whipped Tofu
with Pickled Shiitake

This can be a meal in itself, perfect for a very hot day, but is also an amazing side salad. For the ground shiitake mushrooms, I stick dried mushrooms in a spice grinder or blender to form a fine powder. It makes a dressing that clings to the kohlrabi, adding deep pops of umami to a zippy, crunchy salad. If you can't find kohlrabi, you can make this with finely shredded white cabbage.

Serves 4
—— *Vegan*

1.2kg (2lb 11oz) kohlrabi (about 3 or 4) (or see recipe introduction)
1 tablespoon olive oil
1 tablespoon lemon juice
½ teaspoon fine sea salt
15g (½oz) basil leaves, torn
1 tablespoon poppy seeds

For the sesame whipped tofu
290g (10¼oz) silken tofu, drained
1 tablespoon lemon juice
2 teaspoons toasted sesame oil
½ teaspoon agave syrup
½ teaspoon fine sea salt

For the pickled shiitake
1 teaspoon caster sugar
1½ tablespoons soy sauce, or tamari
1½ tablespoons sherry vinegar
15g (½oz) ground dried shiitake mushrooms (see recipe introduction)
3 tablespoons water
10g (¼oz) fresh root ginger, peeled and finely grated
1 tablespoon olive oil
2 teaspoons mirin

For the whipped tofu, put everything in a blender and blitz until totally smooth. Transfer to a container and chill until ready to use.

To make the pickled shiitake, put the sugar, soy, vinegar, mushrooms and measured water in a small saucepan and set over a medium heat. Bring to the boil, then reduce the heat to a simmer for a further minute, stirring continuously, until half the liquid has evaporated and the mushrooms have thickened the sauce.

Transfer this to a small bowl and allow to cool for a few minutes before adding the ginger, olive oil and mirin, whisking to combine.

Peel the kohlrabi, cut it into 5mm (¼-inch) wide batons and place in a large mixing bowl. Add the olive oil, lemon juice, salt and basil and toss to combine.

Smooth the chilled tofu over your serving dish and top with the kohlrabi, leaving the remaining dressing in the bowl, as otherwise it will dilute the tofu. Spoon over the shiitake dressing and sprinkle over the poppy seeds to serve.

Coconut, Cumin & Marmalade Fennel Salad

This looks unassuming, but the dressing is where all the flavour is. I am not a fan of loads of different vegetables in a salad; mostly, I pick one and let it shine. The coconut cream dressing is inspired by a salad I had at Kiln Thai restaurant in Soho, London. Dress it just before serving or the fennel will release a lot of liquid.

Serves 4
—— *Vegan*

800g (1lb 12oz) fennel bulbs (about 3)
150g (5½oz) mixed radishes, finely sliced
2 tablespoons tarragon leaves

For the coconut-cumin dressing
100g (3½oz) coconut cream
2½ tablespoons marmalade
2 tablespoons olive oil
1½ teaspoons fine sea salt
1½ teaspoons ground cumin
finely grated zest of 1 unwaxed lime, plus 2 tablespoons juice
1 garlic clove, roughly chopped
20g (¾oz) desiccated coconut

For the sesame mix
2 tablespoons toasted sesame seeds
1 tablespoon black sesame seeds
1 tablespoon toasted desiccated coconut

Place all the ingredients for the dressing except the desiccated coconut in a blender, ideally a high-powered bullet blender, and blitz until emulsified and smooth. Stir in the desiccated coconut and set aside.

Stir together the sesame mix ingredients in a small bowl and set aside.

Take your fennel and slice off the tops, retaining the fronds for later. Slice the bulbs vertically through the cores. Remove the tough outer layers (these can be saved for a stock). If the bulbs are large and have a tough core, use a knife to cut out a cone-shaped piece at the base. For smaller, more tender fennel, the core can be left intact. Use a mandoline or sharp knife to shave it into thin slivers.

Put the fennel slivers in a large mixing bowl along with the dressing, radishes and half the tarragon. Toss thoroughly in the dressing. Sprinkle over the sesame mix, remaining tarragon and reserved fennel fronds to serve.

—— **How to serve**

There's something so bright and refreshing about this combination, so it's best paired with richer recipes such as Tamarind Pumpkin, Confit Garlic & Orzo (see page 92).

Kale
with Kumquat Dressing & Crispy Shallots

If you haven't come across kumquats before, they are little olive-sized citrus fruit, a bit like oranges, except the whole thing is edible, including the skin. The flavour is more floral than an orange, and they add a really intense citrus taste to recipes. They are available in some major supermarkets, but if you can't track them down, swap them out for the finely grated zest of two unwaxed oranges or three tangerines and 2 tablespoons of their juice.

Serves 4
—— **Vegan**

90ml (6 tablespoons) neutral-flavoured oil
150g (5½oz) banana shallots, halved lengthways and finely sliced into half moons
1 red chilli, halved lengthways, deseeded and finely sliced

For the kumquat dressing
2 garlic cloves, roughly chopped
1½ tablespoons rice vinegar
70g (2½oz) kumquats, roughly chopped, including skins (or see recipe introduction)
1 teaspoon orange blossom water (optional)
1 tablespoon lime juice
½ tablespoon agave syrup
1 tablespoon toasted sesame oil
1 teaspoon fine sea salt
250g (9oz) kale, coarse stalks removed, torn into bite-sized pieces

Put the neutral-flavoured oil in a small saucepan and set over a medium heat. Set a sieve over a small heatproof bowl. Heat the oil to 180°C (350°F) or, if you don't have a thermometer, until it sizzles when you drop in a piece of shallot. Add the shallots and chilli and fry for 5–6 minutes, stirring every so often, until beginning to turn golden and crisp. Use some caution here, as they continue to brown after being strained, so get them to just *before* the point of totally golden.

Tip the contents of the saucepan into the sieve and allow both the oil and solids to cool before transferring the solids to a plate lined with kitchen paper.

Once the oil is cool, put 40ml (2½ tablespoons) of it in a small blender with the garlic, rice vinegar, kumquats, orange blossom water (if using), lime juice, agave syrup, sesame oil and salt and blitz until totally smooth and homogenous. You can also do this with a stick blender.

Put the kale in a large bowl, pour in the dressing and toss to ensure the leaves are completely coated, using your hands to massage the dressing into the kale for at least 2 minutes until it begins to soften and has overall reduced in volume.

Transfer the dressed kale to a serving dish and sprinkle over the reserved crispy chilli and shallots to serve.

On the Side

Cucumber, Rose & Nigella Seed Salad

Lebanese cucumbers are ideal in this recipe, as their flavour is concentrated and they're much crunchier than regular cucumbers, so it's worth tracking them down. If you do use regular cucumbers, they'll need 15 minutes longer when salted to extract as much water as possible. If you're using rose water essence rather than rose water, you'll need to halve the quantity, as it's a lot more concentrated.

Serves 4
—— **Vegan**

800g (1lb 12oz) Lebanese cucumbers, trimmed and cut into 1cm (½-inch) cubes (or see recipe introduction)
1 tablespoon sea salt flakes
1 tablespoon dried rose petals, to serve (optional)

For the mint & rose water dressing
25g (1oz) mint leaves, roughly chopped
6 tablespoons olive oil
4 tablespoons lime juice
½ teaspoon fine sea salt
25ml (1fl oz) rose water (or see recipe introduction)
1 garlic clove, finely grated
1 teaspoon agave syrup
2 teaspoons nigella seeds

Place the cucumbers in a medium bowl, toss with the sea salt flakes, then transfer to a colander set over the bowl. Leave for 20 minutes (see recipe introduction if using regular cucumbers) until some liquid has accumulated in the bowl. Use a clean tea towel to pat the cucumbers as dry as possible before transferring to a clean bowl.

To make the dressing, put the mint, olive oil, lime juice, salt, rose water, garlic and agave syrup in a blender, ideally a high-powered bullet blender, and blitz to a smooth dressing. Add to the cucumbers with the nigella seeds and stir to combine.

Transfer to a serving dish and sprinkle with the rose petals, if using.

—— **How to serve**

While this is a refreshing salad to have on the side of any of the mains in the book, it's also great served over yogurt or Labneh (see page 24) as part of a mezze spread.

Baby Gem, Tamarind Dressing & Avocado Crema

With beautifully crisp baby gem lettuces, this is very loosely based on a wedge salad, but seen through a Persian palate, hence the dill and tamarind. You can make the dressing, croutons and crema ahead of time and just assemble the salad when needed.

Serves 4-6
—— **Can be made vegan**

3 baby gem lettuces, quartered

For the croutons
125g (4½oz) stale crusty bread, cut into 5mm (¼-inch) cubes
3 tablespoons olive oil
1 garlic clove, finely grated
¼ teaspoon fine sea salt

For the tamarind dressing
1 teaspoon tamarind paste
3 tablespoons olive oil
finely grated zest of 1 unwaxed lime, plus 1 tablespoon lime juice
½ garlic clove, finely chopped
2 tablespoons agave syrup, or maple syrup
½ teaspoon fine sea salt

For the avocado crema
2 avocados, destoned, peeled and roughly chopped
200ml (7fl oz) crème fraîche, or vegan alternative
20g (¾oz) dill fronds, plus more to serve
2 tablespoons lemon juice
1 teaspoon fine sea salt

Preheat the oven to 180°C fan (400°F), Gas Mark 6.

For the croutons, toss the bread cubes with the oil, garlic and salt and spread into a single layer over a baking tray. Roast for 15-20 minutes, tossing every 5 minutes or so, until golden and crisp. Allow to cool entirely before using.

Put all the ingredients for the tamarind dressing in a small bowl and whisk to combine.

For the crema, put all the ingredients in a blender and blitz until completely smooth.

Smooth the crema on to your serving dish, add the baby gems, cut sides up, then use a teaspoon to drizzle the dressing over the lettuces. Sprinkle over the croutons and dill and serve.

Burnt Honey, Black Vinegar & Parmesan Radicchio

Bitter leaves require a sweet dressing and the burnt honey and black vinegar add so much to this midwinter salad. Sadly, there's no real substitute for black vinegar, which is often labelled Chinkiang vinegar. It's a great ingredient to have in your cupboard. Regular oranges are totally fine here in lieu of blood oranges.

Serves 4
—— *Can be made vegan*

1 head of radicchio, separated into leaves
1 endive, separated into leaves
60g (2¼oz) lamb's lettuce, or rocket
leaves from 30g (1oz) mint
2 blood oranges, segmented (see page 128)
20g (¾oz) Parmesan cheese, or vegan alternative, finely grated

For the burnt honey dressing
3 tablespoons honey, or agave syrup
2 teaspoons Chinkiang black vinegar
2 teaspoons soy sauce, or tamari
½ teaspoon fine sea salt
¼ teaspoon sweet smoked paprika
1 garlic clove, finely grated
1 tablespoon olive oil

Start by caramelizing the honey for the dressing. The trick here is to watch it very carefully and be ready to decant into a heatproof bowl as soon as it reaches the desired colour, as it's easy for this to burn. Put the honey in a small saucepan set over a medium heat, using a spatula to continuously stir, and making sure you have a heatproof bowl close to hand. In 2–3 minutes the honey will bubble up and then turn an amber shade. As soon as the colour has changed, decant it into the bowl. (If the honey is very dark and sets to a solid block, it's too burnt and you'll have to start again.)

Immediately whisk the remaining dressing ingredients into the honey until fully combined and homogenous. Allow to cool completely.

Put the radicchio, endive, lamb's lettuce, mint leaves and oranges in a bowl and toss with the dressing. Add half the Parmesan and toss, then transfer to a serving platter and sprinkle with the remaining Parmesan.

On the Side

Peas, Walnuts & Orange Blossom Water

A dressing containing orange blossom water sounds like it should be reserved for desserts. However, my favourite use of this ingredient is actually in savoury food, where its floral flavour seems to take the astringency out of harsh-tasting vinegar and mustard. In this salad, it's the subtle star of the show, and – rather revelatory – a pea's best friend!

Serves 4
—— *Can be made vegan*

375g (13oz) frozen peas, defrosted and drained
80g (2¾oz) feta cheese, or vegan alternative, roughly crumbled
15g (½oz) mint leaves, roughly chopped, plus more leaves to serve
60g (2¼oz) walnuts, toasted and roughly chopped

For the orange blossom & lime dressing
2 teaspoons orange blossom water
finely grated zest of 1 unwaxed lime, plus 2 tablespoons lime juice
1 tablespoon sherry vinegar
1 garlic clove, finely grated
1 teaspoon agave syrup, or maple syrup
1 tablespoon Dijon mustard
¼ teaspoon freshly ground black pepper
½ teaspoon fine sea salt
2 tablespoons olive oil

Put your peas in a bowl and use a potato masher to lightly crush them. Add the feta and half the mint.

In a little bowl, whisk together all your dressing ingredients until fully combined, then pour over the peas. Stir this all together, transfer to a serving plate and scatter with the chopped walnuts and remaining mint.

Green Beans & Corn
with Hot Sauce & Ras el Hanout

This is quite spicy and tangy in the way that Frank's RedHot sauce is, especially with the addition of lime, with ras el hanout adding complexity. Of course, feel free to sub out Frank's for your hot sauce of choice. I like it here for its pronounced acidity against the sweetcorn, but Cholula would work nicely too. If you like things a little milder, feel free to reduce the quantity of hot sauce a little.

Serves 4
—— *Vegan*

½ teaspoon fine sea salt, plus more to cook the beans
440g (1lb) fine green beans, trimmed and halved
4 tablespoons olive oil
165g (5¾oz) can of sweetcorn, drained
½ red onion, finely chopped
50g (1¾oz) roasted salted peanuts, roughly chopped

For the hot sauce & ras el hanout dressing
3 tablespoons Frank's RedHot sauce
3 teaspoons ras el hanout (for homemade, see page 18)
2½ tablespoons lime juice
1 teaspoon fine sea salt
2 teaspoons agave syrup
2 garlic cloves, finely grated

Bring a saucepan of salted water to the boil, add the beans and cook for 3 minutes. Drain, then run under cold water before patting dry.

Put the oil in a small saucepan and set over a medium heat. Add your sweetcorn along with the ½ teaspoon of salt and fry the kernels for about 10 minutes or until they have turned lightly golden and are beginning to pop, stirring every few minutes. Strain through a sieve set over a heatproof bowl, reserving the oil, and allow to cool for 5 minutes or so.

Put the corn in a large mixing bowl with the green beans, onion and peanuts.

For the dressing, to the reserved sweetcorn oil add all the other ingredients and whisk thoroughly to combine and emulsify. Pour this into your bean mixture, toss so that all the veg is evenly coated in the dressing and transfer to serving plates.

—— **How to serve**

This would be great paired with something a little cooling, such as Harissa Roast Carrots, Mango Labneh & Mint, or as part of a spread of salads with the Coconut, Cumin & Marmalade Fennel Salad and the Cucumber, Rose & Nigella Seed Salad (see pages 122, 170 and 174)

On the Side

Tomatoes
with Pistachio Dukkah Oil

This dish is best made at the height of summer, when you have the pick of the most beautiful tomatoes. I like to choose an array of tomatoes to mix it up with different colours and shapes. I'm not ashamed to say I give their stems a good sniff before buying; a sweet, ripe tomato smells very earthy. No smell, no deal. Feel free to swap out the pistachios for whichever nuts you have. I just like pistachios for their emerald green colour against the red.

Serves 4
—— *Vegan*

1kg (2lb 4oz) heritage tomatoes
15g (½oz) purple basil leaves, to garnish

For the pistachio dukkah oil
60g (2¼oz) shelled unsalted pistachios
1 teaspoon cumin seeds, lightly ground
2 teaspoons fennel seeds, lightly crushed
1 tablespoon toasted sesame seeds
2 teaspoons Aleppo chilli flakes
8 tablespoons olive oil
2 teaspoons agave syrup, or maple syrup
4 teaspoons soy sauce, or tamari
½ tablespoon sherry vinegar, or red wine vinegar
1 teaspoon sea salt flakes

For the dukkah oil, pulse-blend the pistachios and cumin, fennel and sesame seeds in the small bowl of a blender, ideally a high-powered bullet blender, then blitz to form a very coarse rubble. Transfer to a bowl and stir in the remaining dukkah oil ingredients.

Cut your tomatoes into jaunty, rough 5cm (2-inch) pieces; it doesn't really matter too much, though the more exposed edges there are, the more surface area the dukkah oil can cling to.

Spread your tomatoes across a large platter and drizzle over the pistachio dukkah oil. Scatter over the purple basil before serving.

Something Sweet

Chocolate, Soy & Olive Oil Torte

I came across Honest Toil olive oil when we first opened Bubala, and it really stood out. The owners, Tom and Juli, who live in Greece, have since become long-term pen-pals. I share my recipes using their oil, they share updates about the olive harvests, I feel connected to what I am cooking with and it's just quite lovely. I sent them this recipe to try and it received their seal of approval. Adding soy sauce to this torte has a very subtle effect: more savoury than lightly salted.

Serves 12

125ml (4fl oz) olive oil, plus more for the tin
125g (4½oz) 70% cocoa solids chocolate, broken into small pieces
125g (4½oz) ground almonds
125g (4½oz) caster sugar
1½ tablespoons soy sauce, or tamari
1 teaspoon vanilla extract
¼ teaspoon sea salt flakes
3 eggs, at room temperature

Preheat the oven to 160°C fan (350°F), Gas Mark 4. Oil a 24cm (9½-inch) springform cake tin and line with nonstick baking paper.

Put the chocolate in a heatproof bowl and place over a small saucepan of simmering water, making sure the bowl does not touch the water. When the chocolate has melted, take the bowl off the heat and whisk in the olive oil, almonds, sugar, soy, vanilla and salt until combined.

Carefully separate the eggs. Whisk the yolks into the chocolate mixture.

In a separate bowl, whisk the egg whites into stiff peaks. Taking one-third of the whites at a time, slowly fold into the chocolate mix until thoroughly combined.

Transfer the mixture to your prepared tin, then bake for 20-25 minutes until the edges of the cake feel firm to the touch. A skewer inserted to the middle will come out slightly sticky, as the cake should remain unset in the middle, which will give you a fudgy texture when it cools. Allow to cool before removing from the tin and serving.

Salted Cinnamon, Pistachio & Dark Chocolate Cookies

You've got pistachio in two ways here: in the dough, giving a background nuttiness, but also in the centre of the cookie, so when you take a bite there are so many textures going on. The result is extremely joyous. I like to freeze the cookie balls before baking, then defrost them and bake one or two at a time for a post-dinner treat. It's an absolute power move. To make the pistachio cream, a high-powered blender – such as a bullet blender – is needed or you won't achieve the luxurious texture desired.

Makes 9

For the dough
65g (2½oz) pistachio cream (see below, or introduction)
90g (3¼oz) unsalted butter, softened
160g (5¾oz) light brown soft sugar
60g (2¼oz) caster sugar
1 egg, lightly beaten
180g (6oz) plain flour
½ teaspoon bicarbonate of soda
100g (3½oz) 70% cocoa solids chocolate, chopped
large pinch of sea salt flakes

For the pistachio cream (or see recipe introduction)
120g (4¼oz) shelled unsalted pistachios
¼ teaspoon sea salt flakes
2 teaspoons ground cinnamon
3 tablespoons neutral-flavoured oil
2½–3 tablespoons milk
1 teaspoon agave syrup, or maple syrup

For the pistachio cream, bring a saucepan of water to the boil, add the pistachios and simmer for 5 minutes, then drain. The skins should come off easily with a squeeze, but to speed things up you can put the pistachios in a clean tea towel and rub them lightly to dislodge the skins.

Place the skinned pistachios in a high-powered bullet blender with the salt and cinnamon and pulse-blend until you have a crumb. Add the oil, then blitz. Scrape down the sides of the blender a few times in between blending bursts. The mixture doesn't need to be completely smooth at this stage. Remove 65g (2½oz) of this and place in a large mixing bowl for later.

To finish the pistachio cream, add the milk 1 tablespoon at a time and blend, scraping down between bursts, until you have a creamy paste as smooth as your blender can make it. Transfer to a bowl and stir through the agave syrup, then chill to firm slightly while you make your dough.

In the large mixing bowl, mix the reserved pistachio mixture, butter and sugars until well combined but not creamed; about 1 minute. Add the egg and whisk until smooth, scraping down the sides of the bowl to make sure it is all incorporated. Stir in the flour and bicarbonate of soda until a smooth dough forms. Add your chocolate and salt and stir again until evenly distributed.

Weigh the mixture into 9 × 75g (2¾oz) pieces, roll each into a ball and place, evenly spaced, on 2 baking trays lined with nonstick baking paper. Flatten each ball with the palm of your hand until about 9cm (3½ inches) in diameter and place 1 teaspoon of pistachio cream in the middle. Once all the cookies are topped with the cream, bunch up the edges to reform each ball, roll it lightly in your hand to ensure it's all sealed, then place it back on the tray, seam facing down. Freeze the dough balls at this stage, if you like (see recipe introduction).

Preheat the oven to 165°C fan (365°F), Gas Mark 4½.

Bake for 12–14 minutes until dark brown at the edges but still soft to the touch in the middle; once they cool they'll set, so be careful not to overbake. Allow to cool for 10 minutes before eating.

No-churn Muscovado Ice Cream
with Ras el Hanout Raisins

This ice cream is slightly chewy from the evaporated milk, and the muscovado gives it a deep molasses flavour. The sherry-soaked raisins need at least two days to plump up and absorb the sherry and ras el hanout flavours, so if time is not on your side, this ice cream honestly pairs with so many other things: candied nuts, a little olive oil, chopped mango or strawberries. To me, this tastes like Christmas.

Serves 8-10

For the muscovado ice cream
410g (14½oz) can of evaporated milk, well chilled
290g (10¼oz) dark muscovado sugar
600ml (20fl oz) double cream
½ teaspoon sea salt flakes

For the ras el hanout raisins
150g (5½oz) raisins
150ml (¼ pint) sherry, rum or brandy
finely grated zest of 1 unwaxed orange
⅛ teaspoon ras el hanout (for homemade, see page 18)

For the raisins, put everything in a jar, seal, shake to combine and leave in the fridge for at least 2 days to macerate.

To make the ice cream, put all the ingredients in a large bowl and whip with electric beaters for 7–8 minutes until the mixture has thickened slightly and all the sugar has dissolved. The mixture won't reach the stage of stiff peaks, but you should be able to see the whisk leaving tracks in the cream and it will look a little paler than it did at the start.

Transfer the ice cream to a 2-litre (3½-pint) capacity container and freeze overnight, or for at least 8 hours.

Remove the ice cream from the freezer 40 minutes or so before you want to serve it, to allow it to defrost a little. Run an ice cream scoop under hot water, then scoop up the ice cream, transfer to serving bowls and spoon over some of the raisins and their syrup.

Za'atar & Cherry Chocolate Fridge Cake Bars

Though very much a dessert, these cake bars are rendered almost savoury by the za'atar, which, teamed with salt, makes them incredibly addictive. Za'atar and chocolate is definitely not a traditional pairing, but the herbal quality from the ground thyme and hyssop works so well with chocolate. However, if the combination scares you, feel free to start by using just ½ tablespoon of za'atar. Either way, the flavour will intensify once chilled.

Makes 8

—— *Can be made vegan*

150g (5½oz) 70% cocoa solids chocolate, roughly chopped
50g (1¾oz) agave syrup, or maple syrup
60g (2¼oz) unsalted butter, chopped, or vegan alternative
1 tablespoon za'atar
¼ teaspoon sea salt flakes
100g (3½oz) glacé cherries, roughly chopped
80g (2¾oz) oat biscuits such as Hobnobs, crumbled into 2cm (¾-inch) pieces
50g (1¾oz) shelled unsalted pistachios, roughly chopped

Line a 450g (1lb) loaf tin with clingfilm, ensuring there is enough overhang to allow you to lift out the bars once they are set.

Put everything except the biscuits and pistachios in a heatproof bowl and set over a saucepan of simmering water, making sure the bowl does not touch the water. Heat gently, stirring regularly, until everything is melted and fully combined. Remove from the heat and stir in the biscuit and pistachio pieces.

Transfer to the prepared tin and press the mixture down until compacted and evenly distributed. Cover with clingfilm and refrigerate for at least 2 hours until fully set.

Pull the set cherry-chocolate slab out of the tin, transfer to a chopping board and remove all the clingfilm. Cut into 8 equal-sized bars to serve.

Zohar Cake

I met Tomer Hauptman in 2014 at my first chef's job at The Palomar. He went on to run a vegetarian pop-up focused on dreamy, freshly made hummus, with the most amazing cake for dessert, which was the last thing I ate at a restaurant before lockdown. I couldn't stop thinking about it afterwards. It's the perfect marriage of a lemon drizzle and *basbousa*, an Arabic semolina cake soaked in syrup. The recipe came with just one caveat: you don't mess with the zohar. So here it is, as Tomer intended.

Serves 8
—— *Can be made vegan*

120ml (4fl oz) olive oil, plus more for the tin
120g (4¼oz) fine semolina
40g (1½oz) plain flour
40g (1½oz) ground almonds
170g (6oz) caster sugar
¼ teaspoon bicarbonate of soda
½ teaspoon baking powder
¼ teaspoon fine sea salt
finely grated zest of 1 unwaxed orange
finely grated zest of 1 unwaxed lemon
120ml (4fl oz) milk, or vegan alternative
120g (4¼oz) yogurt, or vegan alternative
1 teaspoon apple cider vinegar

For the citrus syrup
80ml (2¾fl oz) orange juice (1 orange)
4 tablespoons lemon juice (1 lemon)
100g (3½oz) caster sugar
½ teaspoon orange blossom water

Preheat the oven to 175°C fan (380°F), Gas Mark 5. Oil a 24cm (9½-inch) springform cake tin and line with nonstick baking paper.

Put the semolina in a medium-sized bowl with the flour, ground almonds, sugar, bicarbonate of soda, baking powder, salt and zests and whisk thoroughly to combine.

Put the 120ml (4fl oz) of oil in a separate large bowl with the milk, yogurt and vinegar and whisk thoroughly so that there are no lumps. Add the dry mixture to the wet and whisk only until combined; over-whisking could toughen the crumb. Spoon the batter into the prepared cake tin.

Bake for 30–35 minutes until golden and a knife comes out clean once inserted.

Meanwhile, combine the juices and sugar for the syrup in a small saucepan and set over a medium heat. Simmer for 7–8 minutes until you have an amber-coloured syrup. You can test the consistency by spooning a little on to a plate and dragging your finger through it: if it doesn't run back, it's ready. Turn off the heat and stir in the orange blossom water.

As soon as the cake comes out of the oven, evenly pour over the syrup and let it cool completely before removing from the tin and slicing.

—— **How to serve**

This is lovely served with ice cream or sorbet: vanilla would be lovely, pistachio sublime, almond even better. Or, quite simply, just serve with yogurt or crème fraîche, or a vegan alternative.

Earl Grey, Halva & Blackberry Fool

Four teabags may seem like a lot, but you really want the bitterness of the tea here to offset the rich cream. You can find halva at Middle Eastern grocers, or sometimes at supermarkets. However, failing that, stir 75g (2¾oz) tahini together with 75g (2¾oz) honey and ripple this through the cream instead. You'll need to make the infused cream at least four hours before you want this, as the cream needs to be 100 per cent chilled or it won't whip.

Serves 4

300ml (½ pint) double cream
4 Earl Grey teabags
30g (1oz) caster sugar
1 tablespoon cardamom pods, toasted and crushed
1 teaspoon vanilla bean paste
⅛ teaspoon sea salt flakes
200g (7oz) Greek yogurt
150g (5½oz) halva, roughly crumbled (or see recipe introduction)
finely grated unwaxed lemon zest, to serve (optional)

For the macerated blackberries

150g (5½oz) blackberries
1 tablespoon agave syrup, or maple syrup
finely grated zest of 1 unwaxed lemon, plus 1 tablespoon lemon juice

Put the cream, teabags, sugar and cardamom pods in a saucepan and set over a medium heat. Stir and bring to the boil, then turn off the heat and transfer the mixture to a lidded container. Chill in the fridge until completely cold; this will take at least 4 hours.

Tip the blackberries into a bowl with the agave syrup and lemon zest and juice. Stir and set aside.

Pour the infused cream through a sieve into a bowl and discard the solids. Use electric beaters to whip the cream until stiff; this should take around 3 minutes. You can do this with a hand whisk, but it will take much longer. Fold in the vanilla, salt, yogurt and halva to combine.

Transfer the whipped cream to 4 serving dishes and top with the macerated blackberries, then scatter with a little more lemon zest, if you like.

Ice Cream
with Soy Caramel & Maple-Chilli Oil

This is my low-effort entertaining dessert. All you need to do is make the two sauces ahead of time, then just buy the best ice cream you can find. I go for vanilla, but this caramel and oil work equally well with strawberry, or even chocolate. The chilli oil is not overly spicy (in my opinion), so feel free to use more Aleppo chilli and hot paprika, if you'd like.

Makes enough to serve 4

460ml (16¼fl oz) tub of shop-bought ice cream (see recipe introduction)

For the soy caramel
50g (1¾oz) caster sugar
50g (1¾oz) unsalted butter, chopped
100ml (3½fl oz) double cream
4 teaspoons soy sauce
pinch of sea salt flakes

For the maple-chilli oil
5 tablespoons olive oil
2 star anise
1 cinnamon stick
1 tablespoon black sesame seeds
1 tablespoon toasted white sesame seeds
¼ teaspoon hot smoked paprika
½ tablespoon Aleppo chilli flakes
2 tablespoons maple syrup
pinch of sea salt flakes

To make the soy caramel, place the sugar in a small saucepan and set over a low heat, swirling the pan occasionally so that the sugar catches evenly and resisting the urge to go in there with a spoon until it's fully melted. At this point, grab a rubber spatula (wooden spoons are too hard to clean of the caramel) and stir it. Remove from the heat, add the butter and cream and stir rapidly until the butter is fully melted and combined.

Return the mixture to the heat and stir continuously until it begins to bubble. Turn off the heat and stir in the soy and salt, then decant into a heatproof container and allow to cool.

For the maple-chilli oil, put the oil into a saucepan along with the star anise and cinnamon and bring to a gentle simmer over a low heat for 4–5 minutes until aromatic. Turn off the heat and allow to cool for 10 minutes.

Find a small, heatproof bowl and tip in the remaining maple-chilli oil ingredients. Pour the oil over the sesame seed mix, stir, then allow to cool fully.

To serve, scoop the ice cream into serving bowls. Spoon the soy caramel over the ice cream first, then scatter with a little of the maple-chilli oil to taste.

Chocolate Mousse, Passion Fruit & Black Lime Salsa

This method is a revelation, which I first discovered from the king of vegan baking, Phil Khoury. I couldn't believe that simply whisking plant-based milk and chocolate could create such an incredible velvety texture, akin to a *crémeux*. It needs at least four hours to set in the fridge, and I'd also invest in good-quality chocolate as, due to the simplicity of the recipe, there's very little to hide behind.

Serves 6
—— **Vegan**

550ml (1 pint) unsweetened plant-based milk, well chilled
200g (7oz) 70% cocoa solids vegan chocolate, roughly chopped
100g (3½oz) 85% cocoa solids vegan chocolate, roughly chopped
2 tablespoons maple syrup, or agave syrup
⅛ teaspoon fine sea salt

For the passion fruit & black lime salsa
125g (4½oz) passion fruit pulp (3 passion fruit)
25ml (1fl oz) olive oil
40g (1½oz) cacao nibs
2 tablespoons maple syrup, or agave syrup
½ teaspoon Aleppo chilli flakes
2 tablespoons lime juice
1 teaspoon black lime powder

Pour 300ml (½ pint) of the milk into a pan, set over a medium heat and bring to the boil. Put both chocolates and the maple syrup in a jug wide enough to use a stick blender in. As soon as the milk comes to the boil, pour it over the chocolate, leave to sit for 30 seconds to allow the chocolate to melt, then blend with your stick blender until well combined and glossy. Add the remaining milk – ensuring it is fridge-cold – and salt, then blend again until combined.

Pour the mixture into a container and lay clingfilm directly over the surface. Chill for at least 4 hours until set. This whole process can also be done in a stand-alone food processor if you don't have a stick blender.

Stir together all the ingredients for the salsa in a bowl.

To serve, divide the passion fruit salsa between shallow bowls. For each portion, warm a spoon under hot water, dry it, then scoop out a serving of the mousse and place on top.

Carrot & Lemongrass Halwa

At Bubala, we rotated the duty of making the staff meal through all the chefs in the kitchen and it was my favourite part of the day. I was forever amazed by the talent, effort and love my chefs poured into feeding their colleagues. Salonee Patel's staff food was always knock-out, drawing from her Indian heritage but with her own unique spin. On one memorable day, she *also* treated us to dessert, which was usually impossible given how pushed we were for time. She made a halva similar to this… and I won't forget the moment of calm as members of staff sat and ate the rare treat in rapturous silence.

Serves 8–10
—— *Can be made vegan*

12 cardamon pods, toasted and lightly crushed
800g (1lb 12oz) carrots, peeled and coarsely grated
2 × 400ml (14fl oz) cans of coconut milk
2 lemongrass stalks, lightly crushed
1 cinnamon stick
1 teaspoon grated nutmeg
60g (2¼oz) raisins
80g (2¾oz) unsalted butter, or vegan alternative
6 tablespoons caster sugar
¼ teaspoon fine sea salt
2 teaspoons rose water
2 teaspoons tamarind paste

For the rose cream
100ml (3½fl oz) double cream, or vegan alternative
100g (3½oz) Greek yogurt, or vegan alternative
1 teaspoon rose water

To serve
30g (1oz) toasted cashew nuts, finely chopped
30g (1oz) shelled unsalted pistachios, toasted and finely chopped

Place the cardamom pods in the centre of a small square of muslin and tie it into a bundle with string (this is so that you don't have to struggle to pick them out of the mixture later). Place the bundle in a large saucepan. Add the carrots, coconut milk, lemongrass, cinnamon, nutmeg and raisins.

Bring the mixture to the boil, then reduce the heat to a medium simmer and cook for 50 minutes, stirring regularly, or until the liquid has evaporated and the carrots are beginning to catch on the bottom of the pan. Stir more often as it reaches the end of the cooking process, to avoid burning the halwa. Add the butter and sugar, stir to combine and cook for a further 8 minutes, again stirring regularly, until the carrot is looking glossy and translucent.

Turn off the heat and stir in the salt, rose water and tamarind paste. Allow to cool for 15 minutes or so then remove the muslin bundle from the saucepan, along with the lemongrass stalks and the cinnamon stick.

For the rose cream, put the cream, yogurt and rose water in a bowl and whip gently for a minute or so until it thickens.

Spoon your halwa into bowls, top with the rose cream and sprinkle over the chopped nuts.

Tahini & Date Caramel Apple Terrine

I like to bring out this recipe for Rosh Hashanah, the Jewish New Year, when you traditionally eat apples and honey to conjure sweetness in the year ahead. It feels quite elegant for the low level of effort needed *and* is gluten free. You can use honey or agave syrup if you don't have date syrup, and vegan butter also works in lieu of regular butter.

Makes 8 slices
— **Can be made vegan**

80g (2¾oz) unsalted butter, or vegan alternative
1 tablespoon ground cinnamon
50g (1¾oz) date syrup
70g (2½oz) tahini
½ teaspoon sea salt flakes
1kg (2lb 4oz) Braeburn apples (about 4)

Preheat the oven to 180°C fan (400°F), Gas Mark 6.

Set a saucepan over a medium heat and melt the butter gently. Pour it into a mixing bowl and whisk in the cinnamon, date syrup, tahini and salt until the mixture is thoroughly combined.

Peel the apples, then use a mandoline (or sharp knife) to shave each as finely as possible up to the cores, which you can discard.

Line a 450g (1lb) loaf tin with nonstick baking paper. I tear a large sheet, crumple it into a ball, then unfurl it, pressing it into the tin so that it comes all the way up the sides, allowing you to pull the terrine easily out of the tin later.

Pour a little of the caramel into the bottom of the prepared tin, then layer in your apples, ensuring they slightly overlap, as this will help you pull the terrine out of the tin later. As you go, use a pastry brush to coat each layer in the caramel, repeating until you have used up all the apples. Pour any remaining caramel over the top, then fold over the baking paper to ensure the top is covered.

Place in the oven for 1 hour; the terrine is ready when you can easily slide a knife through it.

Allow to cool for 1 hour, then chill overnight, adding a couple of cans to the baking paper-covered top of the tin to press the terrine lightly.

When you're ready to serve, transfer the terrine to a chopping board and slice it into 8. For a little more drama, you could place it on a platter in the middle of the table.

— **How to serve**

I love eating the leftovers for breakfast the next morning with a bit of yogurt. It also isn't that sweet, so pairs well with ice cream, or whipped sweetened cream.

Malabi
with Sumac Strawberries & Black Sesame Brittle

Consider a *malabi* the Middle East's answer to panna cotta. It is served in all sorts of ways, depending on where you're eating it; here it is given a British spin for a take on the classic strawberries and cream. Malabi has to be made ahead of time, as it needs at least three hours to set, plus the brittle needs time to cool and the strawberries time to macerate.

Serves 4-6

350ml (12fl oz) whole milk
300ml (½ pint) double cream
80g (2¾oz) caster sugar
1 teaspoon vanilla bean paste
40g (1½oz) cornflour
1 tablespoon rose water

For the black sesame brittle
50g (1¾oz) caster sugar
2 teaspoons black sesame seeds, lightly toasted
2 teaspoons white sesame seeds, lightly toasted
2 teaspoons desiccated coconut, lightly toasted
¼ teaspoon sea salt flakes

For the sumac-macerated strawberries
300g (10½oz) strawberries, hulled and cut into 5mm (¼-inch) slices
1 tablespoon lemon juice
½ tablespoon sumac
½ tablespoon icing sugar

To make the malabi, put the milk, cream, sugar, vanilla and cornflour in a saucepan. Set over a medium heat and whisk continuously until the mixture starts to thicken and the whisk leaves trails as it moves through the mixture; this should take 4-5 minutes. As soon as it thickens, stir in the rose water, whisk thoroughly until completely smooth, then strain into a dish measuring about 20 × 15cm (8 × 6 inches), using a spatula to push the mixture through the sieve. Place a sheet of clingfilm or nonstick baking paper directly on the surface. Transfer to the fridge to chill and set for at least 3 hours.

For the brittle, first lay a sheet of nonstick baking paper on a baking tray and keep this to hand. Put the sugar in a small saucepan and set over a medium heat. Swirl the pan about occasionally to help the sugar caramelize evenly; this will take about 3½ minutes. Once most of the sugar has melted, you can come in with a spatula and give it a little stir until it has all dissolved and the sugar is a dark amber colour. Add the sesame seeds, coconut and salt. Stir so that these are evenly distributed before scraping out the mixture on to the lined tray. Try to smooth the mixture into a flat, even layer, but don't worry too much, as you'll chop it up later anyway.

Allow the brittle to cool uncovered for 1 hour before chopping. I like a mix of large chunks and fine powder.

Put all the ingredients for the strawberries in a bowl and stir to combine. Cover and allow the strawberries to macerate for at least 2 hours.

To serve, spoon the malabi into bowls, spoon the strawberries and their juices alongside, then sprinkle over the black sesame brittle.

Rhubarb, Raspberry & Marzipan Crumble

I've seldom met a crumble I didn't like, and this iteration with marzipan tossed into the crumble mix is particularly fun. I buy frozen raspberries from the supermarket for this and just defrost them before using. They may be a little less perfect than fresh berries, but this doesn't matter when you cook them all down in the filling.

Serves 6

For the marzipan crumble
120g (4¼oz) ground almonds
50g (1¾oz) icing sugar
1 egg white
½ teaspoon almond extract
pinch of sea salt flakes
140g (5oz) self-raising flour
70g (2½oz) unsalted butter, cold and roughly cubed
20g (¾oz) golden caster sugar
60g (2¼oz) blanched hazelnuts, roughly chopped

For the rhubarb & raspberry filling
400g (14oz) rhubarb, trimmed and cut into 1cm (½-inch) slices
500g (1lb 2oz) raspberries (see recipe introduction)
40g (1½oz) golden caster sugar
1 teaspoon vanilla bean paste
4 tablespoons lemon juice
30 twists of black pepper
1½ tablespoons cornflour
pinch of sea salt flakes

To make the crumble, put the ground almonds, icing sugar, egg white, almond extract and sea salt flakes in a bowl and use your hands to bring it together into a ball of marzipan. Wrap this in clingfilm and pop in the freezer for 15 minutes.

Preheat the oven to 170°C fan (375°F), Gas Mark 5.

Tip the flour into the same bowl you used for the marzipan, add the cubed butter and use your fingers to rub it into coarse crumbs. Stir in the caster sugar with a fork, then take your chilled marzipan and use your fingers to crumble it into rough teaspoon-sized balls, adding it straight into the flour mix. Use your fingers to lightly crumble this again, as you did when you added the butter, into coarse crumbs.

Put all the ingredients for the filling in a bowl and toss to combine. Transfer to a baking dish measuring about 24cm (9½ inches) in diameter, spreading it into an even layer. Top with the crumble mix, again ensuring it's in an even layer (there will be gaps, but this is totally fine). Sprinkle over the hazelnuts.

Bake for 45–50 minutes until the crumble is golden and the fruit bubbling. Set aside to cool slightly before serving.

How to serve
This is perfect served with cream, ice cream or custard.

Hot Apricots & Cold Saffron Custard

What is deeply enjoyable here is the contrast of the cold saffron-infused custard against the hot, burnished, slightly bitter apricots. For maximum impact, I'd recommend making the custard at least three hours ahead to allow it enough time to chill, and you can also cut your apricots ahead of time and store them in the fridge. Then all that's left to do is to fry the apricots just before serving.

Serves 4

2 tablespoons olive oil
320g (11¼oz) ripe apricots, pitted and quartered
2 tablespoons maple syrup
pinch of sea salt flakes

For the saffron custard
pinch of saffron threads
1 tablespoon freshly boiled water
300ml (½ pint) double cream, at room temperature
3 egg yolks, at room temperature
45g (1½oz) caster sugar
½ teaspoon vanilla bean paste

To make the custard, first 'bloom' the saffron by grinding it to a powder with a pestle and mortar. Add the measured boiling water, stir, then leave for 10 minutes.

Pour the bloomed saffron and its liquid into a medium-sized saucepan. Add the cream, egg yolks, sugar and vanilla and whisk thoroughly to combine. Set over a very low heat and cook for 10–15 minutes, stirring continuously with a spatula, until the custard has thickened and coats the back of a spoon. If you have a food thermometer, it should reach a temperature of 80°C (176°F). Strain the custard through a fine sieve if it's looking lumpy, then transfer it to a bowl and cover the top directly with a sheet of clingfilm to prevent a skin from forming. Place in the fridge until cool.

Once ready to eat, set a pan over a high heat and add the olive oil. Add the apricots and fry for 5–6 minutes, tossing regularly, until slightly caramelized. Add the syrup and salt and toss so that the apricots are all coated, then transfer to a bowl along with the juices.

Divide the cold custard between serving bowls and spoon over the hot apricots.

Poppy Seed & Orange Blossom Babka

Two of my very good friends, Barclay and Karol, run an amazing vegan pop-up between London and Warsaw called Bracia, meaning 'brothers' in Polish. They aren't actually brothers, but they may as well be. They are two of the most beautiful and inspiring souls I've met. Their Polish sensibility resonates with my Eastern European heritage, and for this book they wanted to contribute a dish that speaks of our shared roots... which could only mean poppy seed *babka*. In their words: 'Tear it with friends, family members, lover(s) or just eat the whole thing by yourself... Whatever. *Smacznego!*'

Makes 1 loaf
—— *Vegan*

For the brioche
260g (9¼oz) strong bread flour, plus more to dust
5g (⅛oz) fast-action dried yeast
5g (⅛oz) fine sea salt
20g (¾oz) white caster sugar
160ml (5¾fl oz) high-protein soya milk (with just soya and water on the label)
65g (2¼oz) Naturli vegan block butter, soft and roughly cubed
a little neutral-flavoured oil

For the poppy seed tahini filling
65g (2¼oz) poppy seeds
65ml (2¼fl oz) water
125g (4½oz) tahini
60g (2¼oz) date syrup
¼ teaspoon fine sea salt

For the orange blossom syrup
50g (1¾oz) caster sugar
25ml (1fl oz) water
¾–1 teaspoon orange blossom water, to taste

To make the brioche, put the dry ingredients in the bowl of a stand mixer fitted with the dough hook and whisk them together.

Gently warm the soya milk in a small saucepan until it reaches body temperature: place your finger in the milk, and when it no longer feels cold but doesn't feel warm, it's ready. Pour the soya milk into the dry ingredients and use your hook attachment to knead the dough for 2 minutes. You may need to scrape any leftover dry ingredients from the bottom of the bowl and incorporate them in the dough.

Now add the butter gradually, in cubes, waiting until each has been incorporated before adding the next. Then knead for a further 5 minutes; the dough should be smooth. Take the dough out of the bowl and knead with your hands for a final 2 minutes, then shape it into a ball.

Lightly oil a clean bowl, add the dough, cover with a damp cloth and leave to rise for 1–1½ hours until doubled in size, then chill it overnight for at least 8 hours. It will continue slowly to rise a little and develop flavour in the fridge.

To make the filling, use a pestle and mortar or spice grinder to lightly crush the poppy seeds. Tip them into a small saucepan with the measured water and bring to a gentle simmer, then simmer for 3–5 minutes until all the water is absorbed before setting aside to cool.

—— *continued overleaf*

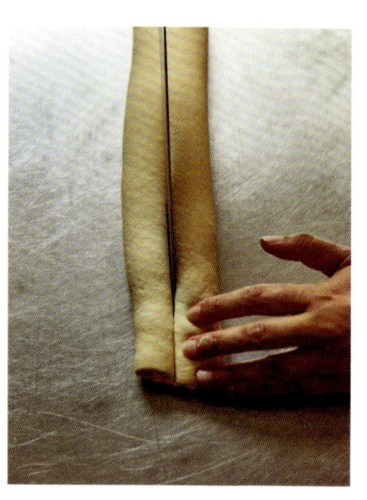  

Put the tahini in a bowl with half the date syrup and mix thoroughly; it will begin to thicken. Then mix in the remaining date syrup and the salt. Once the poppy seeds have cooled, stir them through the tahini mixture, adding 1–2 tablespoons more water to loosen it slightly; you want it to resemble thick peanut butter in consistency.

Once the dough has risen, roll it out on a lightly floured surface into a rectangle about 40 × 35cm (16 × 14 inches), with a long edge facing you. Spread your poppy seed mix evenly over the surface, leaving a 2cm (¾-inch) border on all sides to prevent the filling from spilling out. Starting from the long edge, roll the dough up tightly into a log.

With the seam side facing down, use a sharp knife to halve the log lengthways all the way through, exposing the layers. Turn the cut sides upwards and gently twist the 2 strands together into a loose plait, keeping the exposed layers facing up as much as possible.

Line a 900g (2lb) loaf tin with nonstick baking paper, then carefully transfer the plait into it, tucking the ends under slightly if needed. Cover and set aside to rise again for a further 1–1½ hours until puffy before baking.

To make the syrup, combine the caster sugar and measured water in a small saucepan. Set over a medium heat and stir gently until the sugar has fully dissolved. Once the syrup is clear and just starting to simmer, remove from the heat, stir in the orange blossom water and let it cool completely.

Preheat the oven to 180°C fan (400°F), Gas Mark 6.

Bake the babka for 20 minutes or until golden and risen. Remove from the oven, cover tightly with foil and bake for a further 12 minutes. Take it out of the oven, remove the foil, pour over the cooled orange blossom syrup as evenly as possible, then leave to cool in the tin.

UK/US Terms

UK	US
Aubergine	Eggplant
Baking paper	Parchment paper
Barbecue	Grill
Bicarbonate of soda	Baking soda
Biscuits	Cookies
Blanched nuts	Skinned nuts
Caster sugar	Superfine sugar
Celeriac	Celery root
Chilli flakes	Red pepper flakes
Chinese leaf	Napa cabbage
Clingfilm	Plastic wrap
Coriander (herb)	Cilantro
Cornflour	Cornstarch
Courgette	Zucchini
Desiccated coconut	Shredded unsweetened coconut
Fast-action dried yeast	Instant yeast
Green/red peppers	Bell peppers
Grill	Broiler/broil
Ground almonds	Almond flour
Hob	Stove top
Icing sugar	Confectioner's sugar
Kitchen paper	Paper towels
Marmite	Yeast extract
Muslin	Cheese cloth
Plain flour	All-purpose flour
Plait/plaited	Braid/braided
Rapeseed oil	Canola oil
Rocket	Arugula
Self-raising flour	Self-rising flour
Sieve	Strainer
Spring onions	Scallions
Stem ginger	Preserved ginger
Stick blender	Immersion blender
Strong bread flour	Bread flour
Tea towel	Dish cloth
Tin	Pan
Tomato purée	Tomato paste
The Great British Bake Off	The Great American Baking Show

Vegan Recipes

The Essentials
Ras el Hanout (page 18)
Preserved Lemons (page 18)
Hawaij (page 19)
Baharat (page 19)

The Meal Before the Meal
Caramelized Courgette Dip with Dates & Fenugreek (page 22)
Confit Tomatoes, Hawaij & Crispy Basil (page 26)
Peach, Curry Leaf & Coconut (page 27)
Moutabal & Lime Leaf Dressing (page 33)
Hummus (pages 36–7)
Má là Oil (page 40)
Simple Sesame Oil (page 41)
Rosemary, Caraway & Ancho (page 41)
Matbucha with Jalapeño & Coriander (page 42)
Lahoh (page 44)
Tahini Sauce (page 46)
Basil Zhoug (page 47)
Grated Tomatoes (page 47)
Cumin Aubergine & Coriander Chutney with Star Anise Caramel (page 48)
Curry Leaf & Sumac Ezme (page 51)
Courgette Skewers with Preserved Lemon & Hot Sauce (page 52)
Caramelized Pomegranate Aubergine with Lime Tahini (page 58)
Sesame Chinese Leaf Skewers (page 61)
Pickled Aubergines & Tahini (page 62)
Leek, Miso & Mango Chutney Skewers (page 67)
Mushroom Skewers with Tamari & Pomegranate (page 74)
Dill, Pea & Barberry Fritters with Pomegranate Dip (page 76)
Black Lime & Sichuan Pepper Courgette Fritti (page 79)
Beetroot, Black Garlic & Lime Leaf (page 83)
Roast Watermelon, Silken Tofu & Crispy Onions (page 84)
Hoisin & Coriander Seed Celeriac Skewers (page 88)

Recipes that Can Be Made Vegan

— The Main Event
Tamarind Pumpkin, Confit Garlic & Orzo (page 92)
Courgettes, Peanut Tahini & Pickled Fennel (page 97)
Lemongrass Parsnips with Curry Leaves (page 103)
Pilpil-style Roast Cabbage with Shiitake & Preserved Lemon (page 106)
Carrots, Lime Tahini & Pumpkin Seed Salsa Macha (page 109)
Roast Cauliflower, Saffron Tahini & Cranberry-Chilli Oil (page 116)
Whole Roast Celeriac with Miso Onion Gravy (page 124)
Hispi Cabbage, Whipped Sesame Tofu & Double Ginger (page 127)
Whole Roast Swede & Peanut with Grapefruit (page 128)
Baharat Ratatouille with Preserved Lemon (page 134)
Butternut Squash & Pilpelchuma with Charred Corn (page 137)
Leeks & Kiwi Salsa Verde with Chipotle Pecans (page 143)

— On the Side
Black Garlic & Lemon Pilaf (page 148)
Magic Rice (page 150)
Toasted Buckwheat Tabbouleh (page 153)
Hawaij Roast Potatoes with Preserved Lemon Roast Shallots (page 159)
Ful Medames, Harissa Roast Tomatoes & Pickled Chilli Salsa (page 162)
Okra & Curried Onions with Barberry Dressing (page 167)
Kohlrabi & Sesame Whipped Tofu with Pickled Shiitake (page 168)
Coconut, Cumin & Marmalade Fennel Salad (page 170)
Kale with Kumquat Dressing & Crispy Shallots (page 173)
Cucumber, Rose & Nigella Seed Salad (page 174)
Green Beans & Corn with Hot Sauce & Ras el Hanout (page 183)
Tomatoes with Pistachio Dukkah Oil (page 184)

— Something Sweet
Chocolate Mousse, Passion Fruit & Black Lime Salsa (page 203)
Poppy Seed & Orange Blossom Babka (pages 214–17)

— The Meal Before the Meal
Garlic Butter Malawach (page 28)
Wild Mushroom & Wakame Chilli Crisp with Lime Ricotta (page 64)
Parsnip Chips with Poppy Seed Honey (page 68)
Sweetcorn Ribs, Black Garlic & Chipotle Butter (page 70)
Spiced Farinata with Radicchio & Feta (page 80)
Lime & Ras el Hanout Peppers with Chive Ricotta (page 86)

— The Main Event
Celeriac & Curried Burnt Butter (page 98)
Marzipan Cauliflower with Caraway Oil (page 100)
Leeks, Oregano Butter, Za'atar Feta (page 104)
Roast Broccoli & Curried Sweetcorn Polenta with Jalapeño Oil (page 110)
Flash-fried Mangetout with Hazelnuts & Polenta (page 113)
Hispi Cabbage, Date Butter & Tahini (page 114)
Butternut Squash, Baharat Candied Chestnuts & Whipped Feta (page 119)
Star Anise & Orange Braised Fennel (page 130)
Cauliflower, Bkeila Cream & Sumac Oil (page 132)
Beetroot, Olive & Date Tatin (page 138)
Sweet Potatoes, Amba & Orange Blossom (page 144)

— On the Side
Potato Salad & Basil Zhoug with Coconut Crunch (page 154)
Lime Pickle & Miso Roasted Sweet Potato (page 156)
Amba Butter Beans, Sage & Garlic Crisp (page 160)
Confit Latkes & Soured Cream with Baharat Apple Butter (page 164)
Baby Gem, Tamarind Dressing & Avocado Crema (page 176)
Burnt Honey, Black Vinegar & Parmesan Radicchio (page 179)
Peas, Walnuts & Orange Blossom Water (page 180)

— Something Sweet
Za'atar & Cherry Chocolate Fridge Cake Bars (page 194)
Zohar Cake (page 196)
Carrot & Lemongrass Halwa (page 204)
Tahini & Date Caramel Apple Terrine (page 206)

Index

Amba 14, 144, 160
apples 206
   apple butter 164
apricots, hot, & cold saffron
   custard 212
Ashkenazi egg mayonnaise 56
aubergines 134
   caramelized pomegranate
     aubergine with lime tahini 58
   cumin aubergine & coriander chutney
     with star anise caramel 48
   moutabal & lime leaf dressing 33
   pickled aubergines & tahini 62
   smoked aubergine, harissa & basil
     lasagne 120
avocado crema 176

Baharat 19, 119, 164
   baharat ratatouille with preserved
     lemon 134
barberries 76, 167
basil 26, 120
   basil zhoug 47, 154
beans
   amba butter beans, sage & garlic
     crisp 160
   ful medames, harissa roast
     tomatoes & pickled chilli salsa 162
   green beans & corn with hot sauce
     & ras el hanout 183
beetroot
   beetroot, black garlic & lime leaf 83
   beetroot, olive & date tatin 138
black vinegar 14, 179
blackberries
   Earl Grey, halva & blackberry fool 199
broccoli, roast, & curried sweetcorn
   polenta with jalapeño oil 110
butter 29, 98, 104
   black garlic & chipotle butter 70

butternut squash 137
   butternut squash, baharat candied
     chestnuts & whipped feta 119
   butternut squash & pilpelchuma
     with charred corn 137

Cabbage
   hispi cabbage, date butter
     & tahini 114
   hispi cabbage, whipped sesame
     tofu & double ginger 127
   pilpil-style roast cabbage with
     shiitake & preserved lemon 106
caraway seeds 41, 100
carrots
   carrot & lemongrass halwa 204
   carrots, lime tahini & pumpkin seed
     salsa macha 109
   harissa roast carrots, mango labneh
     & mint 122
cauliflower
   cauliflower, bkeila cream & sumac
     oil 132
   marzipan cauliflower with caraway
     oil 100
   roast cauliflower, saffron tahini
     & cranberry-chilli oil 116
celeriac
   celeriac & curried burnt butter 98
   celeriac skewers 88
   celeriac, Parmesan & Marmite
     fritters 55
   whole roast celeriac with miso onion
     gravy 124
cheese 104, 55, 119, 179
   halloumi & ricotta fritters with
     spiced lemon syrup 73
   lime ricotta 6
   spiced farinata with radicchio
     & feta 80

cherries
   za'atar & cherry chocolate fridge
     cake bars 194
chestnuts 119
chickpeas 34
   hummus 36-7
chillies 14, 41, 162
   black garlic & chipotle butter 70
   butternut squash & pilpelchuma
     with charred corn 137
   chipotle pecans 143
   má là oil 40
   matbucha 42
   wakame chilli crisp 64
Chinese leaf skewers 61
chocolate 190, 194
   chocolate mousse, passion fruit
     & black lime salsa 203
   chocolate, soy & olive oil torte 188
   cinnamon, pistachio & dark chocolate
     cookies 190
coconut 27
   coconut crunch 154
   coconut, cumin & marmalade
     fennel salad 170
coriander 42, 48, 88
courgettes 134
   black lime & Sichuan pepper
     courgette fritti 79
   caramelized courgette dip with
     dates & fenugreek 22
   courgette skewers with preserved
     lemon & hot sauce 52
   courgettes, peanut tahini & pickled
     fennel 97
cranberry-chilli oil 116
cucumber, rose & nigella seed salad 174
cumin 140, 170
   cumin aubergine & coriander chutney
     with star anise caramel 48

curry leaves 14–15, 27, 103
   curry leaf & sumac ezme 51

Dates 22, 114
   beetroot, olive & date tatin 138
   date syrup 15, 206
dill, pea & barberry fritters with
   pomegranate dip 76

Earl Grey, halva & blackberry fool 199
egg mayonnaise 56
evaporated milk 15, 193

Fennel
   coconut, cumin & marmalade
     fennel salad 170
   pickled fennel 97
   saffron-braised fennel, cumin
     yogurt & olives 140
   star anise & orange braised fennel 130
fenugreek seeds 15, 22
flatbreads (lahoh) 44
flatbreads (malawach) 28

Garlic 83, 92, 148, 160
   black garlic & chipotle butter 70
   garlic butter malawach 28
ginger 127
grapefruit 128

Halloumi & ricotta fritters with spiced
     lemon syrup 73
halva
   Earl Grey, halva & blackberry fool 199
   carrot & lemongrass halva 204
harissa 15, 120, 162
   harissa roast carrots, mango labneh
     & mint 122
hawaij 19, 26, 159
hazelnuts 113

hoisin & coriander seed celeriac
   skewers 88
honey 68, 179
hummus 34–6
   toppings 40–1

Ice cream with soy caramel & maple-
   chilli oil 200
ice cream, no-churn muscovado, with
   ras el hanout raisins 193

Jalapeño 42, 110

Kale with kumquat dressing & crispy
   shallots 173
kiwi fruit
   leeks & kiwi salsa verde with chipotle
     pecans 143
kohlrabi & nori crème fraîche with
   pistachio salsa 94
kohlrabi & sesame whipped tofu
   with pickled shiitake 168

Labneh 24, 122
   toppings 26–7
lahoh 44
latkes, soured cream & baharat apple
   butter 164
leek, miso & mango chutney skewers 67
leeks & kiwi salsa verde with chipotle
   pecans 143
leeks, oregano butter, za'atar feta 104
lemongrass 204
   lemongrass parsnip with curry
     leaves 103
lemons 148
   halloumi & ricotta fritters with
     spiced lemon syrup 73
   preserved lemons 18, 52, 106, 134, 159
   zohar cake 196

lettuce, baby gem, tamarind dressing
   & avocado crema 176
lime leaves 83
   moutabal & lime leaf dressing 33
limes 15
   black lime & Sichuan pepper
     courgette fritti 79
   lime & ras el hanout peppers with
     chive ricotta 86
   lime pickle & miso roasted sweet
     potato 156
   lime ricotta 64
   lime tahini 58, 109
   passion fruit & black lime
     salsa 203

Má là oil 40
malabi with sumac strawberries
   & black sesame brittle 208
mangetout, flash-fried with
   hazelnuts & polenta 113
mango chutney 67, 122
Marmite 55
matbucha with jalapeño & coriander 42
miso 67, 124, 156
moutabal & lime leaf dressing 33
mushrooms 106
   mushroom skewers with tamari
     & pomegranate 74
   pickled shiitake 168
   wild mushroom & wakame chilli
     crisp with lime ricotta 64

Nigella seeds 15, 174
nori crème fraîche 94

Okra & curried onions with barberry
   dressing 167
olives 140
   beetroot, olive & date tatin 138

Index —— 221

onions 84, 150, 167
   curry leaf & sumac ezme 51
   miso onion gravy 124
   roast shallots 159
   spring onion salsa 127
orange blossom water 15–17, 144, 180, 214

Pantry items 14–17
parsnips
   lemongrass parsnips with curry leaves 103
   parsnip chips with poppy seed honey 68
passion fruit & black lime salsa 203
pasta 92
peach, curry leaf & coconut 27
peanut butter 97, 128
peas
   dill, pea & barberry fritters 76
   peas, walnuts & orange blossom water 180
pecans 143
peppers 134
   curry leaf & sumac ezme 51
   lime & ras el hanout peppers with chive ricotta 86
   matbucha 42
pistachios 94, 184, 190
polenta 110, 113
pomegranate molasses 17, 51, 58, 74, 76
poppy seeds 68
   poppy seed & orange blossom babka 214–17
potatoes
   hawaij roast potatoes with preserved lemon roast shallots 159
   potato salad & basil zhoug with coconut crunch 154

pumpkin
   tamarind pumpkin, confit garlic & orzo 92
   pumpkin seed salsa macha 109

Radicchio 80
   burnt honey, black vinegar & Parmesan radicchio 179
ras el hanout 18, 86, 183, 192
   ras el hanout raisins 193
rhubarb, raspberry & marzipan crumble 211
rice
   black garlic & lemon pilaf 148
   magic rice 150
rosemary, caraway & ancho 41

Saffron 17, 116, 212
   saffron-braised fennel, cumin yogurt & olives 140
sage & garlic crisp 160
salted cinnamon, pistachio & dark chocolate cookies 190
sauces 46–7
sesame oil 41, 168, 173
   sesame Chinese leaf skewers 61
Sichuan pepper 40, 79
spiced farinata with radicchio & feta 80
spinach 132
star anise 48
   star anise & orange braised fennel 130
strawberries 208
sumac 17, 51, 132, 208
swede, whole roast, & peanut with grapefruit 128
sweet potatoes
   lime pickle & miso roasted sweet potato 156

sweet potatoes, amba & orange blossom 144
sweetcorn 110, 137, 183
   sweetcorn ribs, black garlic & chipotle butter 70

Tabbouleh, toasted buckwheat 153
tahini 17, 97, 116
   lime tahini 58, 109
   tahini & date caramel apple terrine 206
   tahini sauce 46, 62, 114
tamarind 82, 176
tofu 127, 168
   roast watermelon, silken tofu & crispy onions 84
tomatoes 134
   confit tomatoes, hawaij & crispy basil 26
   curry leaf & sumac ezme 51
   grated tomatoes 47
   harissa roast tomatoes 162
   matbucha 42
   tomatoes with pistachio dukkah oil 184

Vegan fish sauce 17

Wakame chilli crisp 64
walnuts 180
watermelon, roast, silken tofu & crispy onions 84

Yogurt 140
   labneh 24–7

Za'atar 104
   za'atar & cherry chocolate fridge cake bars 194
zohar cake 196

Thanks

Thank you to my amazing team at Octopus. To my commissioning editor Louisa – you're such a radiant ball of positivity. To Leanne, for all the meticulous edits; to creative director Jonathan, for your endless patience and skill; and to Ailie and Erin, for getting the word out with such energy and enthusiasm. Thanks to Claire for the gorgeous cover. And thank you to Isabel Jessop for commissioning the book – it's so sad that you didn't get to see it through, but I am so, so grateful for the opportunity.

Thanks to the INCREDIBLE creative team who made this book so beautiful. Yuki, I feel like I won the lottery with you – your talent blows me away. Amazing Emily, you brought my food to life so perfectly. Eden – wholesome queen – you are a joy. Thank you to Natoora who supplied all the beautiful veg you see in the book, and to Poppy for being so generous. Thank you to my one true olive oil supplier Honest Toil who sorted me out with litres and litres of the stuff to test this book – you guys are the best. Thank you also to John Julian for the beautiful props.

To Bruno, for creating a loving and secure environment for me when I was pitching initially, and for listening to the proposal at least 20 times while pacing thoughtfully, giving feedback each time as if it were the first. To Sean – what a journey we've been on together. I am so proud of us. Thank you for all the emotional support. Dani – thank you for putting up with the mess and keeping me sane. Deli – thanks for tasting everything with such dedication, and even throwing a dinner party with the dishes for a group feedback session. Thanks to Zari, who tested a huge chunk of these recipes, as well as all my other friends who cooked them in their homes. To Kate and Jack, who would receive daily parcels of my testing. Your thoughtful feedback helped to shape this book so much.

Thank you to Cressida, my agent – you're amazing. And to Jay Rayner – your support for me and this book has meant so much more than I could express.

Above all, thank you to my family, for always backing me, even with all the seemingly highly questionable life choices that have lead me to this point.

About the Author

Helen Graham is a celebrated chef and food writer based in London. Drawing on her Jewish diasporic roots, she pioneers innovative vegetable-forward cooking inspired by cuisines across the Middle East, Eastern Europe and North Africa.

She has worked at several prominent Middle Eastern restaurants including The Palomar, The Barbary and the Ottolenghi Test Kitchen. Helen was Executive Chef at renowned London vegetarian restaurant Bubala for five years, helping take the business from pop-up to two critically acclaimed sites before leaving in 2023 to go solo.

In 2022, Helen was selected as a rising star by Jay Rayner, and she made her debut television appearance on *Sunday Brunch*. Her recipes have appeared in *Great British Chefs*, *House & Garden*, the *Guardian*, *Vogue*, *Delicious* magazine, *Ocado Life* magazine, the *Financial Times* and the *Observer*.

First published in Great Britain in 2026 by Hamlyn,
an imprint of Octopus Publishing Group Ltd,
Carmelite House,
50 Victoria Embankment,
London EC4Y 0DZ
www.octopusbooks.co.uk

An Hachette UK Company
www.hachette.co.uk

The authorized representative in the EEA is Hachette Ireland, 8 Castlecourt Centre, Dublin 15, D15 XTP3, Ireland (email: info@hbgi.ie)

Text copyright © Helen Graham 2026

Distributed in the US by Hachette Book Group,
1290 Avenue of the Americas, 4th and 5th Floors,
New York, NY 10104

Distributed in Canada by Canadian Manda Group,
664 Annette St., Toronto, Ontario, Canada M6S 2C8

All rights reserved. No part of this work may be reproduced or utilized in any form or by any means, electronic or mechanical, including photocopying, recording or by any information storage and retrieval system, without the prior written permission of the publisher.

Helen Graham asserts the moral right to be identified as the author of this work.

UK ISBN: 978-1-783-25665-5
US ISBN: 978-1-783-25654-9
UK eISBN: 978-1-783-25655-6
US eISBN: 978-1-78325-666-2

A CIP catalogue record for this book is available from the British Library.

Printed and bound in China.

10 9 8 7 6 5 4 3 2 1

Acquired by: Isabel Jessop
Commissioning Editor: Louisa Johnson
Creative Director: Jonathan Christie
Senior Editor: Leanne Bryan
Copyeditor: Lucy Bannell
Cover Designer: Claire Rochford
Photographer: Yuki Sugiura
Food Stylist: Emily Kydd
Props Stylist: Charlie Phillips
Assistant Production Manager: Lisa Pinnell